Reacting against the [barcode] on display in much [...] us have retreated into preaching that is intellectually rigorous but somehow a bit arid, and certainly not fashioned to incite our hearers to repentance, faith, and joyful obedience. Josh Moody and Robin Weekes want to retain the rigor while going after the heart – not 'heart' in the contemporary sense, but in the biblical sense, aligned with what Jonathan Edwards calls the 'affections'. Moody and Weekes encourage us to preach to the affections – not simply the emotions, but the very center of our being, everything that inclines us to think and act and move, and not merely learn. For some, this little book will be a healthy reminder; for others, it will revolutionize their preaching.

D. A. Carson
Research Professor of New Testament
Trinity Evangelical Divinity School, Deerfield, Illinois

This book will be a great help to many who, like me, have begun to be more aware of the importance of preaching to the heart, but have not always quite known how to do it. It is reassuring in its reaffirmation of the importance of faithful exegesis and avoidance of sentimentality, challenging in pushing us to work harder where many preachers have been weak, and really helpful in the practical wisdom it offers. It has not only convinced me of the importance of preaching to the affections, but has also inspired me to think that I must and can do this better.

Vaughan Roberts
Rector of St Ebbe's, Oxford and President of the
Proclamation Trust, London

Moody and Weekes offer a wise reminder that the truth of a sermon – no matter how logically and accurately it reflects Scripture – denies the power of the Word if there is no intention to affect the heart of the listener (or if the preacher is not also personally affected by the Word). The ways we are affected by the Word are our witness of its significance. To proclaim truth without an intended impact upon the attitudes and actions of those who hear it suggests either that the Word is without true meaning or we are to receive it without appropriate synchrony of heart and life.

Bryan Chapell
Pastor, Grace Presbyterian Church
Peoria, Illinois

On the first Easter morning two people walking with him had the Scriptures opened up to them by a stranger; so much so that 'the fire burned' within them as in Psalm 39:3. Messrs Moody & Weekes, with plenty of good sense, would encourage us preachers to reach the hearts of our listeners. Do they have all the answers? Possibly not. Are they making a timely point? I think they are.

Dick Lucas
Formerly Rector of St Helen's Bishopsgate, London

'True religion, in great part, consists in holy affections', said Jonathan Edwards. The trouble today is that people don't quite know what those 'affections' are, leaving us with a false choice: emotionalism or woodenness. This book turns on the lights, helping preachers understand how hearts and lives can be affected by truth. I'm thrilled to see this book, handling such an important subject so well.

Michael Reeves
Director of Union and Senior Lecturer
Wales Evangelical School of Theology, Bridgend, Wales

BURNING HEARTS

Preaching to the Affections

Josh Moody

and

Robin Weekes

PT RESOURCES

CHRISTIAN
FOCUS

Josh Moody (PhD, University of Cambridge) is senior pastor of College Church in Wheaton, Illinois. His books include *Journey to Joy*, *No Other Gospel*, and *The God-Centered Life*. For more, visit www.GodCenteredLife.org.

Robin Weekes has pastored churches in Delhi, India and London, UK where he currently serves as the Minister of Emmanuel Church Wimbledon. He has also been involved with training Bible teachers both in North India and through being on the teaching staff of the PT Cornhill Training Course in London. He is married to Ursula, and together they have been entrusted with three young children.

Copyright © Josh Moody and Robin Weekes 2014

ISBN 978-1-78191-403-8

10 9 8 7 6 5 4 3 2 1

Published in 2014
by
Christian Focus Publications,
Geanies House, Fearn, Ross-shire,
IV20 1TW, Scotland, Great Britain
with
Proclamation Trust Resources,
Willcox House, 140-148 Borough High Street,
London, SE1 1LB, England, Great Britain.
www.proctrust.org.uk

www.christianfocus.com

Cover design by
Daniel van Straaten

Printed by
Nørhaven, Denmark

CONTENTS

They said to each other, 'Did not our hearts burn within us while he talked to us on the road, while he opened to us the Scriptures?'
(Luke 24:32)

Introduction

We have a confession to make: we're both British. Okay, so one of us has lived in the U.S.A. for fifteen years, and the other of us lived in Delhi for six and a half years. But we're still British. And as everyone knows, the British are the not the most 'affectional' people. Not only are we British, but we both went to boarding schools (one of us in Essex, the other in Edinburgh). And as everyone also knows, British boarding schools (which, just to confuse our American friends, are called 'public schools') excel in many ways, but are not known to be hotbeds of affections.

So we realise that we are not the two most obvious people on the planet to be trying to write a book on how to preach to people's affections. Indeed, we're writing this book chiefly for our own benefit as we realise how much we have to learn about the place of the affections in our walk with Christ and in preaching Him to ourselves and others. This has nothing at all to do with emotional manipulation which we abhor. It has everything to do with a biblical anthropology which places the heart at the centre of who God has made us. Through preaching the Bible we have become more and more convinced that this is of great importance, and possibly a neglected theme in our generation of Bible-believing Christians. It has not always been so. Previous generations thought a great deal about the centrality of the heart in the Christian life and the need to preach to people's hearts. It may well be that this book is simply a touch on the tiller and part of a growing discussion about the re-discovery of these things.

I (Robin) want to thank Josh for his willingness to work on this book together. Josh has been doubly kind to me in my life. I first met him in 1991 as a very young Christian at university. Josh was two years above me and president of the University Christian Union. I had always had a sneaking suspicion that living flat out for Christ would somehow make life rather dull. Meeting Josh disabused me of that entirely as he modelled that Christ had come to give life in all its fullness. As a busy, older brother, he showed me great kindness and patience. More than twenty years later, with Josh infinitely busier with caring for a large family and an even larger church, I have experienced that same kindness and patience as we have worked on this book together. Thank you, Josh, for taking me on these two times.

As well as Josh, a number of others have been greatly influential in my life. I want to express my gratitude to my parents David and Jean Weekes, Christopher Ash, Mark Ashton, Jonathan Fletcher, Dick Lucas, Mark Dever, David Jackman, John Pearce, Vaughan Roberts, and the other 'three Musketeers,' Anthony Bewes, Paul Bolton and Tim Dossor. I am also grateful to Emmanuel Church Wimbledon, a church I have been privileged to have served in different capacities for fifteen years and counting.

In terms of the book, my thanks are due to the students of the Proclamation Trust Cornhill Training Course in London 2010-2013 who were guinea pigs for some of this material. I also want to thank those who have taken time to read sections of this book and given me helpful feedback, not least Adrian Reynolds and David Jackman, the editors of PT Resources. I also want to express my thanks to and love for my wife Ursula. As you may see, I am not an experienced writer. She is, and has helped me – as she has in countless other ways – learn to write. I dedicate this book (at least my part of it!) to her. But above all, I want to thank the Lord who has given me a new heart, one that is captured by His love. Echoing John Calvin's seal and motto: 'I offer my heart to you, Lord, readily and sincerely.'

I (Josh) want to say that Robin is far too kind and generous towards me, but that's the kind of person he is. There are people with whom it is a chore to work, others with whom it is easy to work, and then there are those few with whom it is a joy. Working with Robin has always been a joy. I delight to hear how his ministry is flourishing, and it is a real pleasure to write this book together.

My list of people for whom I am grateful seems to grow longer each year. Thank you, the people, pastors, staff and elders of College Church for your godly example and faithful commitment to the proclamation of the gospel. Thank you, Gavin Lymberopoulos, for your research assistance. Thank you, Carolyn Litfin, my Executive Assistant, for countless hours of expertise and support. I also want to thank Phil Parker, Simon Barnes, Michael Walker, Tim Hastie-Smith, Pat Blake, Don Carson, Mark Dever, Kent Hughes, Dick Lucas and many, many others. I give thanks for the ministry of Mark Ashton, who was at St Andrew the Great when I was an undergraduate in Cambridge, and for the ministry of Eden Baptist in the same city. In particular, I would like to dedicate this book to Elijah, two weeks old as I write: may you be a prophet of the Word of God. And especially I thank Rochelle. Long ago it was said to me that your wife either halves or doubles your ministry: you have certainly doubled mine. I love doing life with you. Above all, God be praised.

Josh Moody, College Church, Wheaton, Illinois, U.S.A.
Robin Weekes, Emmanuel Church Wimbledon, London, U.K.
February 2014

1

What are affections?

ANOTHER COUNTRY

It was a Sunday. I (Josh) was waiting for the standard post-service handshake with the vicar. The one difference this time was that I had been abroad until recently, flying back to London the day before. I was jetlagged, sleepy and eager to connect again with my home church minister. He had always been a supporter of my involvement with student work at Cambridge, and I knew he would be excited to hear how the work was going in the far-flung corner of the world to which I had temporarily relocated.

The person before me performed the *shake-smile-thank you*.

Now, you have to realise that the culture where I had been was very different from South London. Only a few days before, I was immersed in a place where friends greeted each other on the street with a kiss. The accepted practice between male friends was something like this:

- left hand behind friend's head…
- right hand firmly grasp friend's hand…
- pull head towards you…
- plant kiss on cheek.

This was not how it was done in South London.

The woman in front of me went off glowing after her brief word with the preacher. It was my turn. I looked at him. My left hand moved behind his head, my right hand grasped his right hand, and I tugged with the left hand to bring his head close to mine. The look on his face was one of sheer horror.

'What have they done to him!' was the thought that flashed across his eyes.

We never actually kissed (you will be glad to know). I averted mid-flight like a jumbo jet pulling up from the runway at Heathrow. Proper protocol was resumed.

'Thank you for the sermon,' I said.

Kissing friends as a sign of affection belonged to another country. It is not what we do.

DEFINING 'AFFECTIONS'

What are affections? They are not touching, hugging, kissing, or (even) feeling: *Affections are the movement of our thoughts, feelings and will towards a desired object, person or event. An affection is what inclines us to something (whereas an effect is what results from something). Affections are what move us towards action.*

When we talk about *preaching to the affections*, we do not mean preaching that is sentimental, or touchy-feely, or lacking intellectual rigour or content. That is not preaching to the affections; that is empty-headed preaching. Nor do we mean preaching that is lacking in close attention to the text of Scripture, or that skims over the surface of the passage in order to create an easy emotional high in the hearers.

What are affections?

Affections are more than emotions (though they include them). Affections are defined by their result: they are what happens within someone when action is produced. We all know it is possible to feel something and do nothing about it. We also all know it is possible to think something and do nothing about it. But when our feelings and our thoughts are combined with a decisive will-to-action, then the internal event that generates this movement is called 'affections.'

Preaching to the affections is 'affectional preaching' (not affection*ate* preaching). Preaching to the affections means preaching that targets the heart. And the heart in the Bible is not merely our feelings, nor merely our thinking, but both intertwined; the heart is the centre of who we are.

Because affections are 'what move us towards action,' affections are:

- part of the brain's response to data
- necessary for rational functioning
- no more fallen or sinful naturally than reason
- orientated towards godly desires in the godly person
- not proof in themselves that someone is spiritual

Affections are part of the brain's response to data
When the Bible talks about the heart, it does not mean what most people today mean by the heart. The heart is not the seat of emotions/feelings/passions. It is the place where emotion and reason come together. The heart is the core of the person.

The primary agenda of the Bible is not to map a careful psychology of the inner life. The Bible is first and foremost a book about God and His Word to us. Nonetheless, while we use heart to mean emotions, the Bible uses heart to include emotions *and* thoughts *and* will.

'The fool says in his heart, "There is no God"' (Ps. 14:1), where we might say 'I was talking to myself' or 'I thought to myself,' assuming that such self-talk took place in the brain. The Old Testament word for heart means heart, centre, middle, suggesting that it is referring to the core. Heart includes the personal, emotional, intellectual and volitional (see Exod. 9:12; Judg. 18:20; Deut. 7:17; 1 Sam. 2:35; 1 Sam. 16:7; 1 Kings 3:9). It includes the will, the intellect and feeling (see Mark 2:6, 8; Mark 3:5; Luke 24:32). Heart, combining emotions and thoughts, is the accepted definition today according to the *New International Dictionary of Old Testament Theology and Exegesis* and the *Theological Dictionary of the New Testament*.

We are talking about overlapping sets of feeling and thinking. There is an overlap between what the Bible calls heart and what the Bible calls gut. There is an overlap between what translators from the King James period onwards described as affections and heart, or what they called thinking or mind.

Jesus said, 'You shall love the Lord your God with all your heart and with all your soul and with all your strength and with all your mind' (Luke 10:27). Jesus is not intending to give us a series of precise distinctions about the inner workings of people. Instead He is saying that the first commandment is to love God with absolutely *everything* you have – heart, soul, strength and mind, each of which integrates. These terms are less like distinct categories and more like a Venn diagram of overlapping sets.

Affections are necessary for rational functioning
Even though emotions are integrated with rational functioning, emotions can still disturb clear thinking. Emotions sometimes get in the way of being rational. That is why we do not expect a judge in a court case to be related to one of the parties, why we realise that

we might not be thinking clearly if we have not eaten properly, and why it is typical advice to avoid making any major decisions after a serious bereavement. Physical, hormonal, circumstantial changes can alter emotions, and emotions can cloud reasonable and logical action.

But there is also evidence that *without* emotion our rational capacity would be diminished. People who spend their days and nights dreaming up ways to create artificial intelligence wonder whether our ability to create computers that *think* will be limited by our ability to create computers that *feel*. Even some of the most rationalistic philosophers have agreed. Immanuel Kant, hardly a sentimental man, said that 'nothing great is ever done without passion.' The case of Phineas Gage appears to confirm the interrelation of emotion and reason. In 1848, the construction foreman Gage had a large iron bar driven through his head. Amazingly, he did not lose consciousness, even making a full recovery apart from loss of vision in his left eye. Gage, though, no longer showed appropriate respect for ethical convention. He made decisions that violated his own personal interest. A more recent 'Gage,' Elliot, had a tumour the size of an orange removed from his brain. Elliot also recovered, including mentally, but he became unable to make decisions. Elliot noted that his feelings had changed. While he appeared able to examine logical options, he was not able to come to a conclusion. He lacked the emotional kick to bring him to the point of decision.

The neuroscientist Antonio Damasio examined these and other matters in his book *Descartes' Error*, concluding that emotion, far from interfering with rational function, was essential to it.[1] Similarly, bestselling books like

---

1.   Antonio Damasio, *Descartes' Error* (London, U.K.: Penguin Books, 2005).

Malcolm Gladwell's *Blink* and Sheena Iyengar's *The Art of Choosing* suggest that in certain circumstances – when we have developed expertise – our decisions may be best informed by our affectional responses, rather than in spite of them. For instance, a skilled and trained football player can 'over-think' when he is faced with a shot at a goal, whereas if he follows his well-honed instincts, he may be more likely to score.

The cause of this is the hard wiring of our brains. While no doubt much still needs to be discovered, and some ideas that are now current will be rejected, developments in brain mapping suggest that emotions have a 'low road' and a 'high road.' There is the immediate emotional response (high road), but then that response can become entrenched in our brain as a short cut (or low road). The ability of our brain to form such short cuts can make it very difficult to break addictive behaviours. But it can also mean that learned responses to events over time build a path of affectional wisdom. Perhaps there is a biochemical reality to the old phrase, 'Sow a thought, reap a deed; sow a deed, reap a habit; sow a habit, reap a destiny.'

Reason and emotion are both fallen
Biblically, both reason *and* emotion are fallen.

Consider 2 Corinthians 4:4, 'In their case the god of this world has blinded the *minds* of the unbelievers, to keep them from seeing the light of the gospel of the glory of Christ, who is the image of God.' Or Romans 1:21-25, 'For although they knew God, they did not honour him as God or give thanks to him, but they became futile in their *thinking*, and their foolish *hearts* were darkened. Claiming to be wise, they became fools… Therefore God gave them up in the lusts of their *hearts* to impurity… they exchanged the truth about God for a lie…'(emphasis added). Or 1 Corinthians 1:21, 'For since, in the wisdom of God, the world did not know God through wisdom, it pleased God through the folly of what we preach to save those who believe.' Or 1 Corinthians 8:1-3, '...knowledge puffs up, but love builds up. If anyone imagines that he knows something, he does not yet know as he ought to know. But if anyone loves God, he is known by God.' In his commentary on 2 Corinthians, Paul Barnett even says that 'The Achilles' heel of man is his mind, since he is so prone to intellectual pride, especially in matters to do with religion.'[2]

On the other hand, while reason and emotion are both fallen, it is clear that the Bible expects Christians to exercise self-control. Part of discipline is keeping unwarranted emotions or passions in check. Galatians 5:24, 'those who belong to Christ Jesus have crucified the flesh with its passions and desires.' Passages like that, and hundreds of others, like Philippians 2:12-16 ('...work out your own salvation with fear and trembling, for it is God who works in you, both to will and to work for his good pleasure. Do all things without grumbling or disputing, that you may be blameless and innocent, children of God without blemish in the midst of a crooked and twisted generation, among whom you shine as lights in the world, holding fast to the word of life...'), show that the Christian is called to exercise self-control over what would otherwise be intemperate desires.

If one person will mistakenly consider that his thoughts are sufficient to contain God ('The fool says in his heart, "There is no God"' Ps. 14:1), another will mistakenly do what feels good *because* it feels good (by contrast, 'I discipline my body and keep it under

---

2.   Paul Barnett, *The Message of 2 Corinthians* (Downers Grove, IL: InterVarsity Press, 1988), p. 82.

control, lest after preaching to others I myself should be disqualified' 1 Cor. 9:27).

There *is* a battle. Both reason and feeling must be proactively, energetically, passionately, logically, wrestled into line with God's Word: 'For though we walk in the flesh, we are not waging war according to the flesh. For the weapons of our warfare are not of the flesh but have divine power to destroy strongholds. We destroy arguments and every lofty opinion raised against the knowledge of God, and take *every thought* captive to obey Christ' (2 Cor. 10:3-5, emphasis added).

Some become frustrated when they hear a person say, 'Keep your emotions in line; don't trust your feelings.' 'Should we always trust our reason instead?' they ask. Others are wary of feelings spiralling out of control. You only have to dip into the descriptions of intemperate revivalism like the magnificent (if strange) *Fits, Trances, and Visions* by Ann Taves, to realise that sometimes telling people not to trust their feelings is the right pastoral thing to do![3] *As long as* we also tell people not to always trust their thinking either. Because as alarming as the weird and wonderful world of *Fits, trances and visions* may be, no less alarming – for any Bible-believing Christian – is what developed from the secular rationalism of the Enlightenment to various streams of liberalism today. Some bow before the idol of experience, others bow before the idol of intellect. Both need to repent and worship the God who reveals Himself in His Word, to our hearts, minds, souls and strength – *all* of which are to love Him.

---

3.   Ann Taves, *Fits, Trances, and Visions* (Princeton: Princeton University Press, 1999).

Affections are orientated towards godly desires in the godly person

Godly affections are the vibrant experience of the godly.

Consider the Psalms. Even a cursory reading tells us that God cares how we feel. Remember not every emotion listed in the Psalms is *approved* by God. But the full range (from joy to anger, from depression to peace, from hate to love) is recorded. Emotions are important enough for God to have them included in holy writ. Of course, the Psalms are far *more* than a therapy session where the psalmist lets it all hang out. They are a model of how to coordinate the full range of human emotions to the revelation of God.

For instance, Psalm 42, 'As a deer pants for flowing streams, so pants my soul for you, O God', is usually referenced as a sweet call to desire God. But it is also desperate: 'My soul thirsts for God, for the living God. When shall I come and appear before God? My tears have been my food day and night, while they say to me all the day long, "Where is your God?"… Why are you cast down, O my soul, and why are you in turmoil within me?' So the psalm is not describing a person on a religious *high*; this is someone on a religious *low* longing to renew their sense of connection with God. Being passionate, or affectional, does not mean, then, that if we feel slightly less excited, we must be slightly less holy. 'Hope in God; for I shall again praise him, my salvation and my God,' battling those emotions into line with the truth of God (Ps. 42:1-3, 5).

Another example is Psalm 126. There the tone is uniformly upbeat – or so at first it appears. 'Then our mouth was filled with laughter, and our tongue with shouts of joy.' Such laughter and joy is directed towards mission: 'then they said among the nations, "The LORD has done great things for them."' They were not just having a good time with God; they were celebrating *because* nations all around the world were hearing what great things God had done. And even in that celebration there is a note of realism: 'Those who sow in tears shall reap with shouts of joy' (Ps. 126:2, 5).

A New Testament illustration is Paul. As an ancient Middle-Eastern Jew, some of his expressions of emotion are determined by that background and culture (perhaps including the 'holy kiss' in Romans, 1&2 Corinthians and 1 Thessalonians). Still, Paul's affection is not only a product of his culture, it is a product of the gospel. '… [W]e could have made demands as apostles of Christ. But we were gentle among you, like a nursing mother taking care of her own children. So, being affectionately desirous of you, we were ready to share with you not only the gospel of God but also our own selves, because you had become very dear to us' (1 Thess. 2:6-8).

Sometimes in his letters to the Corinthians, Paul is like a parent who is being driven crazy by his adolescent children with their partying and general mayhem. He is not cold and calculating; he is passionate, and a little unhinged in a good way, like a mum or dad get a little unhinged when a child comes home two hours later than they said and the parents are having nightmares about whether the child has died or not.

Apparently, Paul was emotional enough to cry a fair bit: 'For I wrote to you out of much affliction and anguish of heart with many tears, not to cause you pain but to let you know the abundant love that I have for you' (2 Cor. 2:4). He also blubbed when he was in Ephesus, '…serving the Lord with all humility and with tears' (Acts 20:19), which he wants them to recall when he has gone. 'Therefore be alert, remembering that for three years I did not cease night or day to admonish every one with tears' (Acts 20:31). And when he finally left Ephesus, all the elders let the waterworks flow, and kissed him too, 'And there was much weeping on the part of all; they embraced Paul and kissed him' (Acts 20:37).

That is not the usual way you say goodbye to your vicar.

Some of this is cultural and particular to Paul's own personality. It is as important not to *fake* passion (affect*ation*) as it is to have passion. Ask yourself: what do I do when I am passionate about something *outside* of church life? That may be how I would expect to act when I am passionate about the things of God. If I do not cry when my much loved child leaves home for college, I am unlikely to cry when a missionary leaves for the mission field. But in one way or another, we are to say with Paul, 'I rejoiced in the Lord greatly' (Phil. 4:10), 'sorrowful, yet always rejoicing' (2 Cor. 6:10), 'I am overflowing with joy' (2 Cor. 7:4). Or as Peter put it, 'You believe in him and rejoice with joy that is inexpressible and filled with glory' (1 Pet. 1:8). Or Jesus, 'In that same hour he rejoiced in the Holy Spirit' (Luke 10:21).

Affections are not proof in themselves that someone is spiritual
If it is possible to undervalue affections in the Christian life, it is also possible to overvalue them. The sign of being a Christian, and of making progress as a Christian, is not whether you feel passionately, or express your emotions in ways that appear to others to be passionate. *Salvation* – becoming a Christian – is evidenced by *sanctification* – gradually growing as a Christian. The truth of the gospel is shown by the power of the gospel in changed lives. 'The fruit of the Spirit is love, joy, peace, patience, kindness, goodness, faithfulness, gentleness, self-control' (Gal. 5:22-23). The fruit of the Spirit is *not* weeping, or shouting, or (conversely) being prim and proper. The fruit of the Spirit is *moral change*.

23

What causes this spiritual change is the power of the gospel, the pure Word of God, the seed that goes down into our hearts, and over time gradually produces the fruit of increasing Christlikeness.

In the parable of the sower, Jesus explains, 'As for what was sown on rocky ground, this is the one who hears the word and immediately receives it with joy, yet he has no root in himself, but endures for a while, and when tribulation or persecution arises on account of the word, immediately he falls away' (Matt. 13:20-21). It is possible to have joy, even passionate joy, but for that passion to be short-lived. Simon of Samaria was baptised, 'amazed' at what the apostles were doing, and yet he was not 'right before God' (Acts 8:13, 21). Isaiah chapter 1 shows that religious excitement by itself is not what counts to God; God is looking for godliness of character, 'justice,' doing what is right, that flows from genuine worship of Him.

I remember one person who appeared to be soundly converted, became passionate for the work of the gospel for a season, and now, as far as I know, is nowhere spiritually. Passion may be important, it may be an inevitable part of being human, it may be necessary for good rational function, it may be the fuel for much godly endeavour, but it is not the sign of godliness itself. That is the fruit of the Spirit, perseverance, following Jesus to the end.

Affections then – rightly understood – are part of what it means to be human and are to be increasingly orientated towards godly desires in the Christian. How, though, does preaching relate to affections? To answer that question, we need to make sure we clearly understand what the Bible has to say about proclamation.

2

What is preaching?

The aim of this chapter is neither to replicate nor to contradict much of the excellent material on preaching that is currently available. Instead, we want to focus on a definition of preaching that takes into consideration what we have learnt about the affections in chapter one. Let us restate what we said in the introduction, namely that this has nothing at all to do with emotional manipulation which is something which all preachers must renounce as 'disgraceful' and 'underhanded' (2 Cor. 4:2).

The definition of preaching we will be working from in this book is this: *Preaching is the God-ordained means by which He meets with His people through His Word and by His Spirit in such a way that His people's eyes are opened to see Jesus and be captivated by Him.*

From the outset, we want to make clear that we believe the systematic, continuous exposition of the Scriptures is the most faithful way of preaching the Bible and ought, therefore, to be the staple diet of Christ's church. God gave us books of the Bible, not a handbook of Christian doctrine. That is not to say that there is no room for topical or thematic sermons, although we wonder whether they tend to work best when they are from one Bible passage, such that they are what we might call 'topical exposition.' For example, a sermon on the theme of the authority of Scripture could be well covered by an exposition of 2 Peter 1:16-21. A sermon on the destructiveness of sexual promiscuity and the delightfulness of sexual fidelity could be expounded from Proverbs 5.

Having declared our hand that we believe expository preaching is the queen of sermonic forms, we are aware that people often mean different things by 'expository preaching.' In fact, it is possible to define it in such a way that means there are only a handful of true expository preachers out there. That is manifestly not true. Among the clearest definitions is this: *Expository preaching is where the main point of the passage is the main point of the message.* One of the great encouragements of the last fifty years has been the rediscovery of expository preaching. Under God, in the U.K. this has been due in large part to the ministries of Martyn Lloyd-Jones, Dick Lucas (and The Proclamation Trust[1]), and John Stott (and the Langham Partnership[2]). In other parts of the world, it is thanks to the ministries of many faithful men and churches. We rejoice in this rediscovery and are delighted that there are many outstanding resources for expository preachers today.

DISCOVERING AND DELIGHTING IN GOD

To understand the nature of preaching, we need to realise that the Bible has a single pivotal axis or focus. In Luke 24, the risen Lord Jesus meets with two of His

---

1.　http://www.proctrust.org.uk

2.　http://langhampartnership.org.uk or http://www.johnstottministries.org

disciples on the road to Emmaus and gives them a Bible study. Here's how Luke describes it: 'And beginning with Moses and all the Prophets, he interpreted to them in all the Scriptures the things concerning himself' (Luke 24:27). Notice that according to Jesus, all the Scriptures (which for Him was the Old Testament) are about Him. Whilst we must be careful not to end up with a skewed Christ-centredness that is either forgetful of the Father or neglectful of the Spirit, we must see that Christ is at the heart of Scripture. Theologically that is because God the Son is the One who makes God the Father known to us (see John 1:18 which is in many ways a summary of the theology of John's Gospel). God the Spirit then unites us to the Son in whom we have every spiritual blessing.[3] In other words, Jesus Christ is the hermeneutical key which unlocks every part of the Bible. He is the lens through which all Scripture must be interpreted and lived.[4]

It is fascinating to read how these two disciples describe their experience of Jesus' Bible study with them: 'Did not our hearts burn within us while he talked to us on the road, while he opened to us the Scriptures?' (Luke 24:32). Seeing and meeting Christ in the Scriptures is a profoundly experiential thing. Meeting Christ should affect and transform us. That is confirmed by the way the apostle Paul describes his preaching in Ephesians: 'To me, though I am the very least of all the saints, this grace was given, to preach to the Gentiles the unsearchable riches of Christ' (Eph. 3:8). Notice the content of Paul's preaching – 'the unsearchable riches of Christ.' For Paul, preaching was

---

3. To explore this further, see Christopher Ash's excellent book, *Hearing the Spirit* (Fearn, U.K.: Christian Focus and Proclamation Trust Resources, 2011).

4. See Edmund P. Clowney's helpful book, *Preaching Christ in All of Scripture* (Wheaton, U.S.A.: Crossway, 2003).

about preaching Christ, and preaching all the riches that we have in Him.

The Emperor Jahangir was the ruler of the Mughal Empire in India from 1605 until his death in 1627. Not a man who struggled with low self-esteem ('Jahangir' means 'World Seizer'), he was one of the wealthiest men the world has ever seen. Writing in 1625, Augustine Hiriat, a European jeweller in Lahore, wrote of Jahangir, 'He has a great number of pearls, and it is certain that he also has more large diamonds and large rubies than all the princes of the universe.' In fact, when Jahangir was born, Persian poets likened him to a precious pearl emerging from an oyster. For example, Khwaja Husayn Haravi wrote, 'Praise God, from the prince's might and majesty a pearl of glory from the ocean of justice came to the shore.'[5]

What Jahangir and others aspired to, the Lord Jesus Christ actually is. He came not from the ocean of justice, but from the glory of heaven. He came not from a prince, but from God Himself. He came not to seize the world, but to die for it. More than that, in Philippians 2:6 we're told that although Jesus was in the form of God, He did not 'grasp' equality with Him, but gave it up in order to become a man. As a result, 'God has highly exalted him and bestowed on him the name that is above every name.' That is why Jesus is the 'pearl of great value' (Matt. 13:46). Astonishingly, all those who are 'in Christ' (the New Testament's favourite description of a Christian) share in His riches. That's why the apostle Paul wrote that we have 'every spiritual blessing in the heavenly places' (Eph. 1:3). At the moment, the Lord Jesus is at the right hand of His Father in heaven. One day we will see Him by sight. But until that great day,

---

5. Jahangir, translates Thackston, W.M., *The Jahangirnama* (Oxford, U.K.: OUP, 1999), p. 4.

we see Him by faith as He is revealed in the Bible. Martin Luther (1483-1546) called the Scriptures 'the swaddling clothes and manger in which Christ lies.'[6] It follows then that the aim of Bible reading is to discover & delight in the one true, living God as He is revealed in Jesus Christ. When we read the Bible, we are looking at something – or rather at someone – altogether more valuable, beautiful and glorious than Jahangir or his pearls. As we rejoice that Jesus is *Lord* (Rom. 10:9) and that He is *Saviour* (Luke 2:11), we must not forget that He is also *Treasure*. That's why elsewhere Paul speaks of the 'surpassing worth of knowing Christ' (Phil. 3:8).

However, knowledge of God is unlike all other kinds of knowledge. It is not merely information about a subject or a person, but the revelation of the one true, living God who exists in three persons. Explaining this, Jonathan Edwards (1703-1758) spoke of a two-fold way in which God reveals Himself to people. He wrote:

> God glorifies himself towards the creatures also two ways: (1) by appearing to them, being manifested to their understandings; (2) in communicating himself to their hearts, and in their rejoicing and delighting in, and enjoying the manifestations which he makes of himself... God is glorified not only by his glory's being seen, but by its being rejoiced in, when those that see it delight in it: God is more glorified than if they only see it.[7]

Edwards' distinction here is very helpful. God the Father is glorified when people understand the truth about Him. But He is more glorified when we delight in those truths, or more accurately, when we delight in

6. M. Luther, *The Prefaces to the Early Editions of Martin Luther's Bible* (London, U.K.: Hatchard, 1863), p. 21.

7. Jonathan Edwards, *The Works of Jonathan Edwards, vol. 13 The Miscellanies* (Yale, U.S.A.: Yale University Press, 1994), p. 495.

Him. As John Piper rightly never tires of reminding us, 'God is most glorified in us when we are most satisfied in him.'[8]

THE GOAL OF PREACHING: TO CAPTIVATE PEOPLE'S HEARTS WITH THE BEAUTY OF JESUS

If all the Scriptures are all about Jesus, then the goal of preaching is to captivate people's hearts with His beauty. Here's how the apostle Peter puts it: 'Though you have not seen him [Jesus], you love him. Though you do not now see him, you believe in him and rejoice with joy that is inexpressible and filled with glory, obtaining the outcome of your faith, the salvation of your souls' (1 Pet. 1:8-9). The Christian life is a glorious love affair between Christ the bridegroom and His bride the Church, which means that our aim in preaching should be to engage people's hearts, and not just their minds.

Listen to Jonathan Edwards again:

> I should think myself in the way of my duty, to raise the affections of my hearers as high as I possibly can, provided they are affected with nothing but truth, and with affections that are not disagreeable to the nature of what they are affected with.[9]

If we've forgotten what Edwards means by the affections, look back to chapter one. Edwards here shows why preaching to the affections has nothing at all to do with emotional manipulation. We need to be 'affected by the truth,' not by man-made emotional fervour.

---

8. http://www.desiringgod.org/.

9. C.H. Faust and T.H. Johnson, eds., *Jonathan Edwards* (New York, U.S.A.: Hill and Wang, 1962), p. xxiii.

One of the ways we can do this is by remembering that we are preaching a person, not just teaching a passage. Often in church meetings we hear the leader say something like, 'In just a moment X is going to come and teach the passage that was read to us earlier.' Of course, good preaching will not be less than teaching a passage. Indeed we're commanded to 'rightly handle the word of truth' (2 Tim. 2:15). But it will be – or at least should be – more than that. What we are doing as we preach is presenting Christ, or as the apostle Paul put it, 'Him we proclaim, warning everyone and teaching everyone with all wisdom, that we may present everyone mature in Christ' (Col. 1:28). Christ is the content and the goal of our preaching, but more than that, we actually encounter Christ when the Word of Christ is preached. Commenting on 2 Corinthians 5:20, C.K. Barrett says:

> With the cross, God instituted the office of reconciliation, the word of reconciliation…; in other words, the preaching itself belongs to the event of salvation. It is neither a narrative account of a past event, that once happened, nor is it instruction on philosophical questions; but in it Christ is encountered, God's own word to man is encountered…[10]

Many of the great preachers of the past who stirred people's affections have grasped this well. For example, among John Wesley's advice to preachers was 'to offer Christ' which is a superb way of describing preaching. A century later Charles Spurgeon put it like this:

> Our faith is a person; the gospel that we have to preach is a person; and go wherever we may, we have something solid and tangible to preach, for our gospel is a person. If you had asked the twelve Apostles in

---

10. C.K. Barrett, *The Second Epistle to the Corinthians* (London, U.K.: Black, 1973), p. 178.

their day, 'What do you believe in?' they would not have stopped to go round about with a long sermon, but they would have pointed to their Master and they would have said, 'We believe him.' 'But what are your doctrines?' 'There they stand incarnate.' 'But what is your practice?' 'There stands our practice. He is our example.' 'What then do you believe?' Hear the glorious answer of the Apostle Paul, 'We preach Christ crucified.' Our creed, our body of divinity, our whole theology is summed up in the person of Christ Jesus.[11]

When we have finished preaching, it would be good to ask ourselves, 'Have I just taught a passage? Or have I preached a person?' That's not to set up a contradiction between the written Word of the Bible and the living Word that is Jesus. We must preach the person of Jesus from a passage. And when we do, we will accomplish what J.I. Packer says our aim as preachers should be, namely, 'The proper aim of preaching is to mediate meetings with God'.[12] Preaching then becomes an event, whereby the hearers meet with the living God through the mediator Jesus Christ. Our task as preachers is not to send people away from church saying, 'That was a lovely sermon.' Rather, we want people to leave church saying that they have met with the living God.

We love the way that John Newton, the ex-slave trader and author of the hymn 'Amazing Grace', describes going to church. Writing to his friend John Ryland one Sunday morning, Newton said, 'You must not expect a long letter this morning: we are just going to court, in hopes of seeing the King, for he has promised to meet us.'[13] What

---

11. C.H. Spurgeon, in *Lectures Delivered before the Young Men's Christian Association in Exeter Hall 1858-1859* (London, U.K.: James Nisbet and Co., 1859), pp. 159-60.

12. J.I. Packer, *Truth & Power* (Wheaton, U.S.A: Harold Shaw, 1996), p. 158.

13. John Newton, *Wise Counsel* (Edinburgh, U.K.: Banner of Truth, 2012), letter 15, p. 77.

a wonderful description of going to church – going to the Royal Court to meet with the King! And as Newton knew so well, we meet with Him as His Word is read and preached.

This goal of preaching – to captivate people's hearts with the beauty of Jesus – will mean that affectional preaching is preaching which makes much of Christ. When we read sermons of the past, especially those of the Puritans, we frequently find sermons with titles along the lines of 'the excellencies of Christ.' One of our favourites is by John Flavel (1627-1691) called 'Christ Altogether Lovely'[14] which is an exposition of Song of Songs 5:16. Perhaps one of the reasons we don't often hear sermons like that today is because we have lost sight of the goal of preaching being to lift people's hearts to the beauty of Jesus so that we take greater pleasure in Him than we do in created things.

PREACHING AND TEACHING

I (Robin) remember once having a lengthy discussion with an Indian pastor about whether there was a difference between preaching and teaching. He was arguing that there is a difference, not least because we're told in various places that Jesus taught and preached; for example, 'One day, as Jesus was teaching the people in the temple and preaching the gospel...' (Luke 20:1). Different Greek words are used to describe teaching (*didasko*) and preaching (usually *kerusso* or *euangeliso*). In an attempt to protect the truth that preaching must involve teaching a Bible passage, I argued that there was no difference, that preaching and teaching were one and the same thing, and that Luke here was using the words interchangeably.

---

14. Available here: http://www.iclnet.org/pub/resources/text/ipb-e/epl-10/web/flavel-christ-lovely.html, accessed February 2014.

Whilst the authors of the Bible may use the words 'preaching' and 'teaching' interchangeably (e.g. Luke 20:1, Matt. 11:1, 1 Tim. 5:17), I wonder if my Indian friend was, in fact, right. Preaching, although not less than teaching, is not simply about information impartation. It is about spiritual transformation. It is about mediating an encounter with the living God through His Son in such a way that changes us. Not that the preacher mediates as some kind of priest. Rather, it is the Word which mediates such a meeting.

Exploring this further, Tim Keller discerns four possible subtexts to a sermon. The first is what he calls 'reinforcement' where the subtext of the sermon is, 'Aren't *we* great?' The second is 'performance' where the subtext is, 'Aren't *I the preacher* great?' Whilst those are undoubtedly dangers for all preachers, the third one he identifies is perhaps the one most commonly beneath the surface of many expository sermons, namely 'training,' where the subtext is, 'Isn't this *truth* great?' If the truth is from the Bible, then indeed it is great! But to stop there is to stop at information impartation. Or going back to Jonathan Edwards, it is to stop at the first way that God glorifies Himself: 'by appearing to their understanding.' But when we move from there to the second step – delighting in what God reveals – then we move to Keller's fourth subtext, 'worship': 'Isn't *Christ* great?' This is what God the Father wants from all people – that we worship His beloved Son. And so that is what we want in preaching. That is when we move from teaching to preaching, from information impartation to spiritual transformation.

In an article called *Preaching also to the affections: the need of the hour*, Ian Hamilton shows how this difference is seen in practice. He writes:

I recently heard a comment about two preachers that made me stop and ask myself a serious question.

This was the comment: 'As Mr X's sermon came to a close, he encouraged us to praise and thank the Lord Jesus Christ. When Mr Y finished his sermon my heart was full of praise and thanks to the Lord Jesus Christ.' I think the point the individual was making was this: Mr X's sermon was full of good content; it was instructive, insightful and helpful. Mr Y's sermon was no less instructive; his content was no less good; but it had something Mr X's sermon didn't have - it was 'affectional.' Mr Y sought not only to instruct the mind, he sought, with God's help, to minister to the heart.[15]

In some churches today, expository preaching and indeed small group Bible studies, can sometimes comes across as little more than a comprehension exercise. That is, the preacher or Bible study leader 'understands' the passage and seeks then for his hearers to 'understand' it as well. It is entirely right that we should understand God's Word and work as hard as we can to do so. But to stop there is to stop short. Preaching that takes the affections seriously will move us from merely understanding a passage to meeting a person. Perhaps it is this comprehension-only approach to preaching which results in churches which are doctrinally sound, evangelistically fervent, but where a warm devotion to the Lord Jesus is largely absent. In an address to the Evangelical Ministry Assembly in 2006 called *What's so special about preaching?*, David Jackman diagnosed the problem precisely when he said:

I wonder if we have so over-reacted to the mystical and the subjective-emotional in preaching, that we see it now in terms of dispensing Biblical knowledge rather than pleading with God in prayer and men

---

15. The full article is available here: http://www.banneroftruth.org/ pages/articles/article_detail.php?367. Accessed Feb 2014.

in proclamation to change lives in time for eternity. 'Preach the Word' has become 'Explain the Bible'. There is a difference. Systematic Theology is essential. Biblical Theology in the whole sweep of the Bible's big picture from Genesis to Revelation, in Kingdom and covenant, is deeply enriching. But they are not the way God wrote the Bible and to let them govern the sermon, rather than the text of Scripture as written is to end up speaking about the Bible rather than letting the Bible speak. One is the words of men; the other the Word of God. Not observing the text, but listening to God; not cool analysts, but passionate hearers.[16]

Two pairs of eyes

Ultimately, all of this is a spiritual business. That's why Paul prays for the Christians in Ephesus, 'that the God of our Lord Jesus Christ, the Father of glory, may give you the Spirit of wisdom and of revelation in the knowledge of him, having the eyes of your hearts enlightened, that you may know what is the hope to which he has called you, what are the riches of his glorious inheritance in the saints, and what is the immeasurable greatness of his power toward us who believe, according to the working of his great might that he worked in Christ when he raised him from the dead and seated him at his right hand in the heavenly places' (Eph. 1:17-20). In the Bible's anatomy, each person has two pairs of eyes: one physical and the other spiritual.

Tragically, 'the god of this world has blinded the minds of the unbelievers, to keep them from seeing the light of the gospel of the glory of Christ, who is the image of God' (2 Cor. 4:4). In the recent documentary called *Class of 92* about Manchester United's golden generation of footballers, Eric Cantona said that 'only

---

16. The full address is available here: http://www.proctrust.org.uk/dls/ DavidEMAaddress.pdf. Accessed February 2014.

sport can produce this kind of emotion.'[17] That is the comment of someone who cannot see and experience the glory of Christ. Becoming a Christian is nothing less than having the blind spiritual eyes of our hearts opened so that we can see the beauty of the gospel of the glory of Christ. Growing as a Christian is then about having the eyes of our hearts opened more and more. That is what we should be praying for. And God has ordained preaching as an integral way in which that happens.

We see this in what Paul says in Galatians 3:1: 'It was before your eyes that Jesus Christ was publicly portrayed as crucified.' Of course, the Galatian Christians hadn't *seen* the crucifixion – they weren't eyewitnesses to the death of Christ. And yet Paul thinks that his preaching of Christ crucified to the Galatians was so vivid, so real, that it was as if they had *seen* the crucifixion. Our preaching needs to be no less real. Our aim in preaching should be to engage people's hearts, and not just their minds.

WHAT IS PREACHING?

So to conclude, here's the definition of preaching we will be working from in this book: *Preaching is the God-ordained means by which He meets with His people through His Word and by His Spirit in such a way that His people's eyes are opened to see Jesus and be captivated by Him.*

We hope and pray that this book itself will not simply be information impartation, but will draw us to Jesus and help us to dwell on how altogether lovely He is. Our desire is that this book will stir the affections of those who read it, and enable us to arouse holy affections in others. But how do we do that?

---

17. *Class of 92*, Universal Pictures, Released 2013.

The 'how?' question is linked to the 'why?' question. That is, we'll never think about how to preach to the affections unless we're persuaded that it's necessary. We turn now to thinking about why it is worth preaching to the heart.

3

Why preach
to the affections?

When we are training people to preach, we notice that what is obvious to one group is less so to others and vice versa. There are those for whom preaching to the affections, aiming to engage the whole person through the teaching of Scripture, is assumed to be a normal part of the preparatory process, as well as the goal of delivery. They want their hearts to be engaged with the text, and with the person behind the text, and their hearers not only to 'learn more about the Bible,' but also to encounter the Risen Lord. However, we have found that we cannot assume that everyone immediately agrees that engaging emotions as well as reason is a goal of preaching. While there are those for whom preaching is understood to include preaching to the affections, there are others who are yet to be persuaded that preaching is anything but the impartation of sound information, appropriately exegeted, from the text in front of us.

Here, then, are ten reasons to preach to the affections – reasons that will encourage the already convinced, challenge those who are not persuaded, and perhaps also readjust some of the assumptions that all of us have about what it means to preach to the affections.

REASON ONE: BECAUSE OF BIBLICAL PRECEDENT

Consider Peter's sermon in Acts chapter 2. By the end the listeners are 'cut to the heart' (Acts 2:37). Reading Peter's sermon we discover two precedents for preaching to the affections. First, we discover that Peter is rigorous and careful with his exegesis of Old Testament texts. Given that this is still early in the morning and Peter is preaching what amounts to an impromptu sermon before an unruly crowd before breakfast, we can stand in awe at his Spirit-filled, God-given ability to preach with clarity and biblical content. Second, we are also challenged by the courage he exhibits to tell his hearers that '*you* crucified' Him, specifically to tell them twice (Acts 2:23, 36), and for the sermon to conclude on that note. Peter's hearers were 'cut to the heart' (Acts 2:37) because preaching to the affections from the Bible was the goal of Peter's sermon.

If, like Peter, we exegete a text carefully and with Christological focus, then, like Peter, we will aim for the gospel to be taken to heart.

REASON TWO: BECAUSE OF BIBLICAL WARNING

Jesus warns us about the heart. In Matthew 15 (parallel passage Mark 7), the Pharisees opposed Jesus because their hearts were not right with God. It is not what goes into people that makes them unclean but what comes out of them, that is, out of the '*heart*' (Matt. 15:19/ Mark 7:21). 'This people honours me with their lips, but their heart is far from me; in vain do they worship me, teaching as doctrines the commandments of men' (Matt. 15:8-9/Mark 7:6-7, quoting Isa. 29:13). In Matthew 23:25, Jesus says that the Pharisees clean the outside of the dish but inside, in the heart, they are wrong. Similarly, in Mark chapter 3, Jesus diagnoses resistance to His healing ministry on the Sabbath as not primarily a surface disagreement about the interpretation of various texts, but a profound 'heart' matter (Mark 3:5).

This is not a Pharisee problem; it is the human problem. According to Jesus, *money* problems are really heart problems (Matt. 6:19-24), *marriage* problems are really heart problems (Matt. 19:8), and *discipleship dullness* is really a heart problem as well (Mark 8:17).

Imagine you are on a team playing a game and it comes to half-time. During the break your coach gives a detailed, accurate and insightful analysis of what you are doing wrong and how to correct it. Ignoring the biblical warnings about the heart being the source of our actions and motivations by not preaching to the affections would be a bit like ignoring that half-time talk. Jesus' diagnosis of the heart should lead to an appropriate response of the heart. Jesus' warning about the heart shows us why we are to preach to the affections.

REASON THREE: BECAUSE OF BIBLICAL PROMISE

The *promise* of the Bible (summarising all the biblical *promises*) is fulfilled in the gospel of Christ. Part of that promise is the softness of heart that the gospel is designed to give. Ezekiel 36:26, 'And I will give you a new heart, and a new spirit I will put within you. And I will remove the heart of stone from your flesh and give you a heart of flesh.' The next verse explains the meaning of this promise as follows: 'And I will put my Spirit within you, and cause you to walk in my statutes and be careful to obey my rules' (Ezek. 36:27). Having a 'heart of flesh' is a way of saying that by the Spirit, God's people will follow God's Word.

A ministry of preaching to the affections is a ministry that is aiming to do the gospel work of softening the heart of God's people so that they will follow God's Word. Preaching God's Word with the transforming power of the Holy Spirit softens hearts and changes lives.

We are to preach to the affections because such preaching mirrors the promise of what will take place in the New Covenant. We 'are being transformed into the same image [Christ's] from one degree of glory to another' (2 Cor. 3:18).

REASON FOUR: BECAUSE OF HISTORICAL EXAMPLES

The Puritans are a frequent source for quotations on the affections. Richard Sibbes was called the 'sweet dropper' because of his ability to present the gospel in a gently affecting manner. Jonathan Edwards analysed the significance of *Religious Affections* in his classic book of that name. Edwards' views on affections are familiar within certain theological circles, but it is worth reasserting both his passionate conviction *as well as* his consistent balance. Edwards did not think that simply being excited equated to godliness. He took great pains (over many pages) to clarify exactly what was the fruit of the Spirit in terms of the affective element in Christian discipleship. But not only was he consistently balanced, he was also passionately convinced that affections were essential in Christian ministry and discipleship:

> I am bold to assert, that there never was any considerable change wrought in the mind or conversation of any person, by any thing of a religious nature that ever he read, heard, or saw, who had not his affections moved.[1]

---

1. Jonathan Edwards, *On Religious Affections Vol 1* (Edinburgh, U.K.: Banner of Truth), p. 238.

We wonder whether the affections occupy a similar place of prominence in our ministries. Edwards believed that people in the end do what they want to do *and* what they want to do is formed by what they perceive as desirable. That perception of what is desirable is in turn shaped by many factors all of which are under the sovereignty of God. But the task of the minister of the Word is to call people to genuine heart change by showing them the beauty of Christ.

However, the Puritans did not invent preaching to the affections. The early church preacher John Chrysostom (known as the 'golden-mouthed') also preached with great affective power. Consider this example from Chrysostom's *Homily on Marriage* where he counsels husbands to love their wives as Christ loves the church. Note the affective language he uses to urge husbands to the kind of self-sacrifice the gospel requires:

> And even if it becomes necessary for you to give your life for her, yes, and even to endure and undergo suffering of any kind, do not refuse. Even though you undergo all this, you will never have done anything equal to what Christ has done. You are sacrificing yourself for someone to whom you are already joined, but He offered Himself up for one who turned her back on Him and hated Him. In the same way, then, as He honored her by putting at His feet one who turned her back on Him, who hated, rejected, and disdained Him as He accomplished this not with threats, or violence, or terror, or anything else like that, but through His untiring love; so also you should behave toward your wife. Even if you see her belittling you, or despising and mocking you, still you will be able to subject her to yourself, through affection, kindness, and your great regard for her. There is no influence more powerful

than the bond of love, especially for husband and wife. A servant can be taught submission through fear; but even he, if provoked too much, will soon seek his escape. But one's partner for life, the mother of one's children, the source of one's every joy, should never be fettered with fear and threats, but with love and patience.[2]

There are many examples of great preachers from the past who preached without manipulation or sentimentality but with affective power.

REASON FIVE: BECAUSE OF GLOBAL EXAMPLES

Preaching to the affections is not about 'turning back the clock,' or doing the same as preachers in previous centuries. Preaching to the affections is a phenomenon of the growth of the global church today. Philip Jenkins' book *The Next Christendom* makes the case that the expansion of the church in the southern hemisphere of the globe means that by 2050, only about one-fifth of the world's three billion Christians will be non-Hispanic Caucasian.[3] What can we learn from preaching in other cultures on the subject of preaching to the affections?

Ajith Fernando has been the director of Youth for Christ in Sri Lanka since 1976. In his book *Jesus Driven Ministry*, Fernando explains the 'affective' element that comes along with the nature of the gospel:

The word translated 'gospel' (*euangelion*) in these two verses means 'good news.' This word represents a good summary of what we have said above [about anticipation]. Our task is indeed a wonderfully significant one that should fill us with joy over our call. The

---

2. A selection from *On Marriage and Family Life* by St. John Chrysostom, St. Vladimir's Seminary Press, 1986.

3. Philip Jenkins, *The Next Christendom* (New York: Oxford University Press, 2011), p. 3.

reformer and Bible translator William Tyndale (c.1494–1536) expressed his excitement over the gospel in the preface to his New Testament. He said that the word *gospel* 'signified good, merry, glad and joyful tidings, that makes a person's heart glad, and makes him sing, dance and leap for joy.' Tyndale gave his life for the sake of the gospel at the age of forty-two. Such good news is so important that it is worth dying for.[4]

Fernando then advocates for the recovery of a specific biblical affection that he calls 'groaning':

> The typical growing evangelical church today has a strong theology of the necessity for *growth*....The church also has a strong theology of *praise*...Then our churches have a strong theology of *power* – of God's ability to meet the needs of people and to defeat their foes...But theologies of church growth, of praise, and of power can give rise to serious aberrations if they are not balanced with a theology of groaning.[5]

Fernando explains that this category of 'groaning' comes from Romans 8:23. Groaning can exist with praise; in fact the Bible has a whole literary style called lament in order to help us to give worshipful expression to that groaning. Then Fernando asks why Christians find it hard to be honest with each other about their sins, and seek the mutual help that we need to walk together in godliness. It is, Fernando says, because we have either a defective theology of groaning or a defective category of grace. Instead, we need the two together:

> Defective theologies of groaning and grace can join to cause a church where people are afraid to express their deep hurts and struggles to other Christians. So, for example, when there are problems between members,

---

4.   Ajith Fernando, *Jesus Driven Ministry* (Wheaton, IL: Crossway, 2002), p. 116.

5.   Ibid., pp. 140-41.

they do not talk about it. They do not have the assurance that God's grace is sufficient for this challenge, and they do not have a theology of groaning that can accommodate the temporary unpleasantness that will arise from bringing up the issue. So they choose to ignore it. They continue to praise God and, through concentrating on God's goodness, have satisfying experiences of worship. Because of this emphasis on power, this church will also attract many needy people and thus will grow. Outwardly the leaders may hug and smile at each other, but inwardly there will be hidden frustrations and anger over unresolved problems. They will work together until the problems get so big that they can't bear them anymore. Then they burst out in an unpleasant confrontation. Often the church breaks up, and a group leaves.[6]

Fernando is just one example from the global church of preaching to the affections. No doubt we could also find different cases of preaching from around the world that are emotionally manipulative. The above examples, though, from the global church are balanced and biblical and yet also have an 'affective' element. We can learn from our non-Western brothers.

REASON SIX: BECAUSE OF EVANGELISTIC EFFECTIVENESS
This point is the briefest of the ten because many of the other reasons why we are to preach to the affections overlap with reasons for evangelism. We are not saying that we are to aim to manipulate people's feelings, any more than we think it would be appropriate for us to aim to manipulate their thinking. It is 'our job to preach, God's job to convert.' But preaching is God's method for creating an affective impact upon the hearer's hearts, and conversion is heart change. 'One who heard us was a woman named Lydia, from the city of Thyatira,

---

6.   Fernando, *Jesus Driven Ministry*, p. 143.

a seller of purple goods, who was a worshiper of God. The Lord opened her heart to pay attention to what was said by Paul' (Acts 16:14).

REASON SEVEN: BECAUSE OF PASTORAL WINSOMENESS
Paul's correspondence to the Corinthians gives evidence of the appropriateness, and wisdom, of affectional ministry in relation to pastoral ministry. Paul 'opens his heart' to the Corinthians and asks them to 'open their hearts' to him. 'We have spoken freely to you, Corinthians; our heart is open wide. You are not restricted by us, but you are restricted in your own affections. In return (I speak as to children) widen your hearts also' (2 Cor. 6:11-13). Paul returns again to the theme of openness of heart when he says in chapter 7, 'Make room in your hearts for us. We have wronged no one, we have corrupted no one, we have taken advantage of no one. I do not say this to condemn you, for I have said before that you are in our hearts, to die together and to live together. I am acting with great boldness toward you; I have great pride in you; I am filled with comfort. In all our affliction, I am overflowing with joy' (2 Cor. 7:2-4).

This openness of heart is an example of the appropriateness of affections in pastoral ministry. It is one way of communicating with winsomeness, perhaps especially important in a difficult situation or one of potential conflict. That does not mean that we need to wear our heart on our sleeves. But letting a congregation have a sense of our affection does have apostolic credentials. Affectional pastoral communication can be used by God to bring about healing.

We do need to be careful with 'open heart' communication. David Hansen, in his book on pastoral ministry called *The Art of Pastoring* gives an extended picture of the balancing act of the pastor as an under-shepherd.

According to Hansen, it is healthier for a pastor to aim to be a 'parable' of God's love to his people and avoid becoming a 'symbol.'[7] That is, even in our affectional communication we want to point people to the far greater love of Christ for His people, not end up getting in the way of that love or becoming a surrogate for that love. This affectional pastoral ministry is an art, and it is hard to achieve. Still, with all appropriate caveats, gospel affection expressed in pastoral ministry is a component of pastoral winsomeness.

REASON EIGHT: BECAUSE OF MISSIONAL OPPORTUNITY

When people say 'missional' today, they can mean a number of different ministry approaches. We are simply talking about the task of being in the world, but not of the world. *How* we do that is never easy. As the church becomes contextualised in a situation which is less 'church-y' and more secular, the potential for irrelevance (on the one hand) and compromise (on the other) is great. We do not propose to try to solve contextualisation dilemmas here, or even directly address them; we are just acknowledging that they exist. But in situations where the gospel is being communicated in cultures that are no longer friendly or hospitable to the gospel, we are nonetheless wise to consider the 'affectional' element of communication.

Missiologists have long known this. The story of the 'peace child' illustrates finding a connection point that communicates in the language and culture of a community. You can read about the amazing narrative in Don Richardson's book of that name.[8] Missionaries discovered that there was a tradition embedded in

---

7. David Hansen, *The Art of Pastoring* (Downers Grove, IL: InterVarsity Press, 1994).

8. Don Richardson, *Peace Child* (Glendale, U.S.A.: YWAM/ Regal Books, 1974).

their culture – a 'peace child' – which was intended to function as a way to pacify warring tribes. A child from one tribe was given to another to grow up within the opposing tribe, and functioned thereby as a continual reminder and presence of their new peace. Don Richardson tells the story of how this tribal tradition was used as an illustration of the true peace child who was sent to bring us peace with God. So sometimes also missionaries will talk about speaking the gospel in people's birth language as speaking in their 'heart language.'

Or, consider the phrase 'I do not care how much you know until I know how much you care.' Not that we need *first* to establish affection *before* we are allowed to communicate truth. No, '*always* being prepared to make a defence to anyone who asks you for a reason for the hope that is in you' (1 Pet. 3:15). Still, as people find out how much we care, they are more likely to listen to what it is that we have to say.

REASON NINE: BECAUSE OF THE PURITY OF THE CHURCH

Preaching to the affections maintains the purity of the church. It is insufficient simply to tell people that a certain behaviour or attitude is wrong. We need to know why it is wrong and see affectionally how other behaviours and attitudes are better, sweeter, more wonderful, of more value. The Bible does not only tell us to be holy; it shows us why yearning for holiness is sweet and beautiful. The Bible does not simply tell us to follow God; it narrates the story of the people of God with drama and pathos.

Remember Jesus' encounter with the man with leprosy at the beginning of Mark's Gospel? 'If you will, you can make me clean,' the man says to Jesus (Mark 1:40). Take a moment to picture the scene. A man with a terrible disease, exiled from his people, untouchable, on his knees before Jesus, begging him. Jesus, we know, will heal the man. He is willing. But before He heals him, we are told, 'Moved with pity, he [Jesus] stretched out his hand and *touched* him' (Mark 1:41). The untouchable was touched. Not just that moment, but what that moment revealed – the incarnation – is God's human touch.

We are all surrounded by appeals to our affections. Those in marketing understand that 'beauty appeals' and 'fear repels.' Christians have the greatest beauty to offer. We have the greatest fear from which to run. The purity of the church is advanced through preaching that shows that holiness is *sweeter*.

REASON TEN: BECAUSE OF THE GLORY OF GOD

The ultimate reason why we are to preach to the affections is because heart change honours God and glorifies Him. Ever since Genesis chapter 3, the heart of humanity has been broken by our wickedness and rebellion. Now, on account of the gospel, we are called to 'seek the things that are above...set your minds on things that are above...Let the peace of Christ rule in your hearts...Let the word of Christ dwell in you richly...And whatever you do, in word or deed, do everything in the name of the Lord Jesus, giving thanks to God the Father through him' (Col. 3:1, 2, 15-17).

We hope by now that you're fully persuaded that every preacher should preach to the affections. The question is 'how?' That's where we turn our attention next.

4

How do you preach to the affections?

So far, we have considered what the affections are, what preaching is, and why we need to preach to the affections. In this chapter we want to bring those things together and consider how to preach to the affections.

THE PREACHER AND HIS AFFECTIONS

Anyone who has preached regularly will have no doubt made the alarming discovery that it is hard to take others higher up the mountain than you have already climbed. Thankfully, God in His kindness is able to take people higher through our inadequate preaching. There is great encouragement – not least for the preacher – in the answer to question 55 of the Westminster Larger Catechism:

Q: How does Christ make intercession?

A: Christ makes intercession, by his appearing in our nature continually before the Father in heaven, in the merit of his obedience and sacrifice on earth, declaring his will to have it applied to all believers; Answering all accusations against them, and procuring for them quiet of conscience, notwithstanding daily failings, access with boldness to the throne of grace, and acceptance of their persons and services.

That is good news and freedom for preachers. It means that because of Jesus, even our most inadequate sermon is counted as an accepted service before the throne of grace.

However, the grace of Christ is not an excuse for preaching poor sermons. Humanly speaking, the chief reason why sermons fail to connect with hearers' affections is because the preacher himself has not first had his affections stirred in his preparation. That is why it is crucial that as preachers, we first let God's Word do its work in our hearts, before we think about how it will affect those to whom we are preaching. That is, we need not only to do the hard work on the text – we also need to do the hard work on our hearts. We can always tell the difference between sermons we have preached that have 'gone in' (to our own hearts) before they have 'gone out' to others. The most important part of preaching to the affections therefore is the preacher's own heart.

Our observation is that with the revival in expository preaching, many preachers and Bible teachers realise that they need to give themselves to understanding the text that they are preaching or teaching. As Martin Luther put it so memorably, our responsibility as preachers is to beat your head against the text until it yields.[1] Yet once it has yielded, the hard work is not over. We need then to massage the truth of the text into our own hearts so that God's Word does not simply inform us, but transforms us. Part of the reason why we are less strong in handling our hearts than handling the text is that as classic/

---

1. Luther is probably referring to Romans 1:17, and the 'beating on Paul'. John Piper talks about it in this article: http://www.desiringgod.org/biographies/martin-luther-lessons-from-his-life-and-labor.

conservative/reformed evangelicals, we haven't always been very good at handling our affections. Suspicion of feelings, nervousness about being introspective or intense, and a fear of emotionalism have combined to create a kind of affection-constipation in many. Yet as we saw in chapter one, the affections cannot simply be equated with feelings and dismissed as emotionalism. Right affections are an integral part of an authentic Christian life.

So how do we preach to the affections? Here are some suggestions.

1. Look out for the affections in the text.

Perhaps this will surprise some people, but the Bible is full of affections. However, many times we miss them because the eyes of our hearts are not looking for them. Recently, I (Robin) preached on 2 Corinthians chapter 1. As I was preparing, I read through the whole letter. Granted, the apostle Paul is perhaps at his most affectional in this letter, but even so, I was struck by how frequently he speaks of, and appeals to, the affections. For example, consider again the passage we looked at in chapter three: 'Make room in your *hearts* for us. We have wronged no one, we have corrupted no one, we have taken advantage of no one. I do not say this to *condemn* you, for I said before that you are in our *hearts*, to die together and to live together. I am acting with great *boldness* toward you; I have great *pride* in you; I am filled with *comfort*. In all our *affliction*, I am overflowing with *joy*.' (2 Cor. 7:2-4, emphasis added). Quite apart from Paul's remarkable willingness to die for the troublesome Corinthian church, notice the range of affections he tells them he feels. As we read and re-read the text, let's make sure our eyes are open to the affections that are there.

53

2. *Think Christ, live Christ, apply Christ.*

We saw in chapter one that Jesus Christ is the sum and the substance of the Bible. As such, He is the interpretive key to the whole Bible, which means that whatever part of the Bible we're reading, whether it is Leviticus, Proverbs, Mark or Romans, we should be looking for Jesus. Just as all roads led to Rome, so all texts lead to Christ. Though like with those Roman roads, some texts will lead more directly to Christ than others. Here's how the Puritan author Thomas Adams expressed it:

> Christ is the sum of the whole Bible, prophesied, typified, prefigured, exhibited, demonstrated, to be found in every leaf, almost in every line, the Scriptures being but as it were the swaddling bands of the child Jesus.[2]

We're aware that there is a debate about the extent to which we should be Christo-centric in our reading of the Old Testament, and we must certainly avoid finding Christ artificially in parts of the Bible, or an unbalanced Christo-centricism which ignores either God the Father or God the Holy Spirit. Whichever side of that debate we come down on, all would agree that there should be no limits to our concern to glorify Christ in our preaching.

Some of us may be aware of a helpful approach to interpreting the Bible in terms of three 'Cs': **context** – that is, where does the passage come?; **content** – that is, what does the passage say?; and **consequences** – that is, how does the passage apply? To that, we might helpfully add a fourth and most important 'C' – **Christ**. That is, how does this passage exhibit Christ?

---

2. Quoted in Joel R. Beeke & Randall J. Pederson, *Meet the Puritans: With a Guide to Modern Reprints* (Grand Rapids, MI: Reformation Heritage Books, 2006), pp. xxi-xxii.

Methodologically, Christ would come in between content and consequences. That way we always apply a text once we have interpreted it through the hermeneutical key of Christ.

> Context
>
> Content
>
> **CHRIST**
>
>   Consequences

The advantage of inserting this fourth 'C' of Christ is that it will enhance the probability that we will preach Him, not just about Him or in a way that misses Him altogether. Reflecting on a lifetime of preaching, Sinclair Ferguson urges preachers 'not to lose sight of Christ.' He writes,

> This is an important principle in too many dimensions fully to expound here. One must suffice. Know and therefore preach 'Jesus Christ and him crucified' (1 Cor 2:2). That is a text far easier to preach as the first sermon in a ministry than it is to preach as the final sermon. What do I mean? Perhaps the point can be put sharply, even provocatively, in this way: systematic exposition did not die on the cross for us; nor did biblical theology, nor even systematic theology or hermeneutics or whatever else we deem important as those who handle the exposition of Scripture. I have heard all of these in preaching ... without a centre in the person of the Lord Jesus.[3]

When we 'think Christ,' we will learn to live Him and apply Him. According to the New Testament, the

---

3.   Sinclair B. Ferguson, A Preacher's Decalogue, http://thegospelcoalition. org/themelios/article/a_preachers_decalogue, accessed February 2014.

Christian's life is lived 'in' and 'through' and 'for' and 'under' and 'with' Christ,[4] which means when we are applying Bible passages, we must endeavour to do so by applying Christ. This will keep us from applying the Bible legalistically or morally or abstractly.

3. Probe the workings of the heart

As we saw in chapter one, according to biblical anthropology, we are not made up of head, heart and will. Instead, the Bible says that the heart is the parliament of our lives. Yet in our heart, there are two parts – understanding and inclination. By inclination, we mean that in every human heart there is an instinctive ability to like or dislike something, and to assess its worth. And so our hearts are like heat-seeking missiles, always looking to lock on to whatever they perceive to be excellent. The trouble is, of course, that fallen human hearts naturally lock on to things which are not excellent (such as self-glory) or on to things which are good in and of themselves, but not good if they become ultimate things (such as family or career or ministry). In other words, as John Calvin put it memorably, 'Man's nature, so to speak, is a perpetual factory of idols.'[5] What we need is to see the supreme worth of Jesus Christ, and for our hearts to lock on to Him.

Good biblical preaching then will always probe the workings of the heart. In doing so, it will expose deep-rooted idols and exalt the Lord Jesus. In aiming for the heart, we must remember that the strategy of preaching is not just to move the emotions or the will of the listener, but to illuminate and fire the imagination with

---

4. See John Stott's marvellous book, *Life in Christ* (Eastbourne, U.K.: Kingsway, 1991).

5. John Calvin, *Institutes of the Christian Religion*. 1559th ed. (Westminster John Knox Press, 1960), p. 108.

the truth of the gospel. We must remember that words, including sermons, *do* things to us – and not just on an emotional level. They educate, warn and encourage – not just make me feel happy or sad.

Illustration is a key tool in engaging the imagination, as the preacher evokes mental images in the mind of the listener, especially to make concepts real. The preacher needs to establish the connection between the biblical concept and something we can readily identify with and understand to be true. The art of illustration is the art of incarnating biblical truths in the world in which the audience actually lives. It is a vital component of making the truth spiritually real. Too often, we preachers think of illustration only in terms of stories or anecdotes to illustrate the point we are making. But illustration is far more than that. It is the kind of descriptive language which makes biblical truth not only clear but real.

In order to preach to the heart, we need to understand how the heart works. In particular, we need to understand what Thomas Chalmers called 'the expulsive power of a new affection.' Thomas Chalmers (1780-1847) was a highly influential Scottish theologian and preacher. He was the leader of the Evangelical party at the time of the Disruption in the Church of Scotland in 1843. He once preached a sermon on 1 John 2:15 in which he showed that the best way to expel a wrong affection was by displacing it by a better and right one.[6] Perhaps a practical example will help. Elsewhere, John Piper addresses the issue of lust. Piper writes:

> We must fight fire with fire. The fire of lust's pleasures must be fought with the fire of God's pleasures. If

---

6. The sermon can be read here: http://www.theologynetwork.org/ christian-beliefs/the-holy-spirit-and-christian-living/the-expulsive-power-of-a-new-affection.htm. Accessed May 2014.

we try to fight the fire of lust with prohibitions and threats alone – even the terrible warnings of Jesus – we will fail. We must fight it with the massive promise of superior holiness. We must swallow up the little flicker of lust's pleasures in the conflagration of holy satisfaction.[7]

That example gets us to the heart of what Chalmers is saying:

> There are two ways in which a practical moralist may attempt to displace from the human heart its love of the world – either by a demonstration of the world's vanity, so as that the heart shall be prevailed upon simply to withdraw its regards from an object that is not worthy of it; or, by setting forth another object, even God, as more worthy of its attachment, so as that the heart shall be prevailed upon not to resign an old affection, which shall have nothing to succeed it, but to exchange an old affection for a new one. My purpose is to show, that from the constitution of our nature, the former method is altogether incompetent and ineffectual and that the latter method will alone suffice for the rescue and recovery of the heart from the wrong affection that domineers over it.[8]

So as we probe the heart in our preaching, we are helping people to replace their idols with Christ by setting forth how superior He and His promises are.

4. Preach the pathos as well as the logos of the passage
As a result of the rediscovery of expository preaching as the queen of sermonic methods, preachers recognise the need to preach the logic (*logos*) of the passage. That is, identifying the main idea of the passage and showing

---

7. John Piper, *Future Grace* (Colorado Springs, U.S.A.: Multnomah, 2012), p. 336.

8. See footnote 5, p. 57.

how the parts of the passage contribute to that big idea. This is indispensable. We must never lose sight of the *logos* of a passage. But neither must we lose sight of the *pathos* of a passage, that is that passion or emotion of it. What truths in the text cause us to rejoice? To cry? To be angry? When we get both the logic and the pathos of a passage, we will end up with preaching which is 'logic on fire' (in the words of Martyn Lloyd-Jones). Our sense is that we're better trained to detect the *logos* of a passage than the *pathos*, which may be one reason why sermons can end up being sound but dull.

5. *Learn from those who preach to the affections*

As we mentioned in chapter three, we know that we're not the first or indeed only people to have identified the need to preach to the affections. Standing on the shoulders of giants, we have much to learn from both contemporary preachers throughout the world and preachers of the past. In terms of preachers today, many of the older generation of preachers do this instinctively, and we younger preachers have much to learn from them. In terms of preachers of the past, we have access to many who preached Christ so well to the affections, such as the Puritans. We have much to learn from them. For example, here's Samuel Rutherford in a letter to Lady Kilconquhar on the excellency of Christ:

> 'Put the beauty of ten thousand worlds of paradises, like the Garden of Eden in one; put all trees, all flowers, all smells, all colours, all tastes, all joys, all loveliness, all sweetness in one. O what a fair and excellent thing would that be? And yet it would be less to that fair and dearest well-beloved Christ than one drop of rain to the whole seas, rivers, lakes, and foundations of ten thousand earths.'[9]

---

9.   Bonar, A., *Letters of Samuel Rutherford*, available online at www.ccel.org. The exhortation is itself a quote from Puritan John Flavel (1630-1691) in a sermon entitled 'The fountain of life opened up' available on the same site.

One of the striking things about the Puritans is the way they reached for the highest language to describe the excellencies of Him who is 'distinguished among ten thousand' (Song 5:10), our magnificent Lord Jesus. It reminds us of that line in the hymn 'O Sacred Head, Now Wounded' which asks, 'What language shall I borrow to praise you, dearest Friend?' What a great question! We live in a time when everything is 'great' and 'wonderful' and 'brilliant.' And yet if we use superlatives to describe the mundane, how do we describe the One who is altogether lovely? So here's something we are trying to do: reserve our superlatives for the Saviour. That is to keep the utmost language for our utmost Treasure, and to borrow whatever language we can to praise Him who is.

6. Raise the affections with the truth

Reflecting on what he was doing in preaching, Jonathan Edwards said, 'I should think myself in the way of my duty, to raise the affections of my hearers as high as I possibly can, provided they are affected with nothing but truth, and with affections that are not disagreeable to the nature of what they are affected with.'[10]

In other words, it's not enough in preaching just to get the text right. We must then go the next step and ask, 'In what way do the truths of this text raise my affections and those to whom I am preaching?' It's worth reflecting on the different genres of the sixty-six Bible books. They are not a series of essays but rather contain an enormous range of stories, poetry, drama, and apocalyptic visions. These different genres are all different ways of engaging the hearers' and readers' imaginations and bringing truths home to the heart. At

---

10. C.H. Faust and T.H. Johnson, eds., *Jonathan Edwards* (New York: Hill and Wang, 1962), p. xxiii.

the heart of this is the recurring biblical command to 'remember'. It is remarkable how often God's people in both the Old and New Testaments are called to remember in order to counteract our sinful tendency to forget the Lord.

This forgetting is not usually a matter of intellect and information. We 'forget' the Lord when we lose the sense of the heart of who God is and what He has done. The problem is that the truth we have becomes unreal to us without the God-given means of remembrance. For example, we know that Christ's death forgives us, but due to our sinful nature, spiritually we repeatedly forget. This is why we so often feel unforgiven, even when we are. It is this spiritual remembering that enables us to grow in our love for and likeness to Christ. It is this spiritual remembering that enables us to overcome our sinful tendency to forget.

This is where preaching is so vital to the health of a Christian and the church. For it is the preacher's responsibility to cause us to spiritually remember and to spiritually not forget the glorious realities of the gospel. It is the preacher's responsibility to impress the truth of Christ into his hearers so that the things of Christ are increasingly real to them.

Perhaps an illustration might help. I (Robin) really enjoy cycling. Three times a week I used to cycle from my home in Wimbledon to teach at the Cornhill Training Course in Central London. When I started out, I was very aware of the dangers of cycling in London, but as I became more confident, I became less aware of those dangers. A few months ago I was cycling past Clapham Common and saw an air ambulance had landed there. On the side of the road were a crumpled bicycle and a pool of blood. Every time I cycle past that spot, I remember the dangers of cycling in London. This 'remembering' causes me to ride more carefully!

This idea of spiritual remembering is seen in 2 Peter 1:5-9. Peter instructs his readers to 'supplement your faith with virtue, and virtue with knowledge, and knowledge with self-control, and self-control with steadfastness, and steadfastness with godliness, and godliness with brotherly affection, and brotherly affection with love.' He then says that the person who is lacking in these things has 'forgotten that he was cleansed from his former sins.' Notice that Peter does not say that a lack of growth in character is simply a lack of will power or commitment. Unlike many preachers, Peter doesn't say that his hearers should simply 'try harder.' Rather, he says they have *forgotten* that they were cleansed from their sins. That cannot mean that the people have literally lost mental awareness that they were saved or that they have been forgiven, but rather that they have lost an awareness of the reality of Jesus Christ and His forgiveness. The person and work of Christ is no longer spiritually real to them, and their hearts are no longer locked on to the beauty and truth of Jesus. The way Peter deals with the problem reveals that spiritual growth is mainly a matter of overcoming the tendency to spiritually forget. It is spiritually *remembering* the gospel that truly changes us.

7. Prayer: 'the hour of power'

In chapter one, we noted how ultimately 'seeing' God in His Word was a spiritual issue. It requires nothing less than the power of the Holy Spirit to open our eyes so that we can discover and delight in God, which is why prayer is so important. We are told that the apostles gave themselves 'to prayer and to the ministry of the word' (Acts 6:4). They knew that just the ministry of the Word was not enough. For their preaching to be effective, they needed God to work by His mighty

Spirit. And the way we express our dependence on Him is to do so in prayer. E.M. Bounds was right when he said, 'The preachers who are the mightiest in their closets with God are the mightiest in their pulpits with men.'[11]

How seriously do we take prayer in sermon preparation? We would not dare enter the pulpit under-prepared in terms of the text (because people can spot under-prepared preachers!). And yet many times we have entered the pulpit under-prayed (because no one but God sees that). And yet to preach under-prayed is to preach under-prepared. So we must infuse our preparation with prayer. And we must set aside a time when we pray specifically through the sermon. This is what one friend of ours calls 'the hour of power.' We do this at the stage of having a sermon outline, but before writing it up. That's not the only possible place to have this extended time of prayer, but it's a good place.

As well as praying for those we are preaching to, we need to pray for ourselves as preachers. Here's what the preacher John Newton said in a letter to a friend:

> I trust I have a remembrance in your prayers. I need them much: my service is great. It is, indeed, no small thing to stand between God and the people, to divide the word of truth aright, to give every one portion, to withstand the counter tides of opposition and popularity, and to press those truths upon others, the power of which, I, at times, feel so little of in my own soul. A cold, corrupt heart is uncomfortable company in the pulpit. Yet, in the midst of all my fears and unworthiness, I am enabled to cleave to the promise, and to rely on the power of the great Redeemer.[12]

---

11. E.M. Bounds in *Power Through Prayer* (London, U.K.: Marshall, Morgan and Scott, 1966).

12. *Letters of John Newton* (Edinburgh: Banner of Truth: 1869, 2007), pp. 60-1.

Prayer is the means by which we rely on God's power to be at work in our preaching. That's what Paul means when he writes in 1 Corinthians 2:4, 'my speech and my message were not in plausible words of wisdom, but in demonstration of the Spirit and of power.'

8. Preach with an 'awakened heart'

We began this chapter by noting how crucial our own hearts are as preachers if we are to preach to the affections aright. What is true in our preparation is no less true in our delivery. All preachers would do well to heed this charge from Richard Baxter:

> 'In the name of God, brethren, labour to awaken your own hearts, before you go to the pulpit, that you may be fit to awaken the hearts of sinners. Remember they must be awakened or damned, and ... a sleepy preacher will hardly awaken drowsy sinners. Though you give the holy things of God the highest praise in words, yet, if you do it coldly, you will seem by your manner to unsay what you said in the matter... Speak to your people as to men that must be awakened, either here or in hell. Look around upon them with the eye of faith, and with compassion, and think in what a state of joy or torment they must all be for ever; and then, methinks, it will make you earnest, and melt your heart to a sense of their condition.'[13]

One of the dangers of preaching regularly is that we can lose the sense that preaching is an event where the congregation meets with God, and not just something that happens in our Sunday services. We need to recapture that sense of preaching being the means by which God draws near to His people, and the time when we meet with Him. In order to produce Christians who

13. Richard Baxter, quoted in J. I. Packer, *A Quest for Godliness* (Wheaton, U.S.A.: Crossway, 1990), p. 279.

worship God, we need to have preachers who worship Him first.

SUMMARY

We do not want to give the impression that preaching to the affections is a mysterious art that has only been discovered by a select few. In no way do we want to suggest that there is a two-tier approach to preaching with the 'haves' and the 'have nots.' And yet, we do want to encourage preachers to see the central place the Bible gives to our hearts and our affections, and suggest that expository preaching will be much the richer and have a deeper impact when we more self-consciously take this into account.

5

An Appeal:
Preach to the affections
of our age of affections

OUR CHANGING CULTURE: OPPORTUNITY OR TROJAN HORSE?
This is one of those chapters that we wish we had much
more time to write. That is because the subject is *tricky*
– how, in a relatively short space, do we persuade all
who read this that we are absolutely and unwaveringly
committed to the preaching of the gospel in any and
all ages; and *at the same time* also give an insight into
how culture has changed, and therefore how certain
kinds of preaching are liable to be more effective?
How do we show how to seize the opportunity of
our culture's interest in the affectional element of life,
without allowing that interest to become a Trojan Horse
smuggling in more subjective and unbiblical elements
into contemporary expressions of faith? We really have
no idea. To be honest, it would be much easier simply
to duck for cover.

Perhaps we can start by saying *what we are not saying*.
We are not saying that 'styles' of preaching are value
neutral. This is important to assert because sometimes
we can be too simplistic assuming that *how* we preach

does not influence *what* we are heard to be saying. Our approach to preaching is to be shaped by the message, so that the way we preach – with tender-hearted passion, and rugged commitment to truth-telling – is shaped by the content of the particular passage we are expositing at any particular preaching moment.

Nor are we saying that sometimes it is a good idea to be expository and at other times it is not a good idea. Probably few would get this far in this book and think that we might be saying that we can ditch expository preaching in favour of some other approach. But, again, we are committed to explaining the text clearly, winsomely *and* passionately – in fact our commitment to the text *persuades* us of our need to explain the text clearly, winsomely and passionately. Our commitment to affectional expository preaching is not an *addition* to preaching expositionally, but a necessary result of actually preaching expositorally. How can you explain the glory of the immortal God as Paul indicates in Romans 1:21-25 without yourselves embracing that glory and communicating in such a way that encourages our hearers to be able to join Paul in his joyful 'Amen' at the end of verse 25? A commitment to affectional preaching *comes out of* a commitment to the text of the Bible. It is what the Bible does. It is what the Bible wants us to do as preachers of the Bible.

We are not advocating that preaching should 'go with the flow' in current culture rather than prophetically resist. Some tendencies in contemporary culture are damnable, others are expressions of the ongoing image of God in which we are all made, and reflections of God's general grace and mercy upon all people in all places. A desire then to use a stepping off point in contemporary culture – a bridge – is not saying that we think that everything in that culture is good, or that we should embrace all aspects of any particular contemporary culture, or that affections as perceived in contemporary culture are all good. Surely the desire for a buzz, a thrill, a high, a rush, is *not* all good. But neither is it *all* bad, and there is something in that desire which reflects the heart that is restless until it finds its rest in God. Expository preaching to the affections is aiming to seize that opportunity in the culture and guard against its misunderstanding, by rooting it solidly and lastingly in a commitment to the actual text of the Bible.

As we hope is clear both from this book and our ministries, we are thoroughly committed to the proclamation of the God-centred gospel of Jesus Christ. With God's help we will do that with our dying breath, with our waking groan, with our midnight sigh, in the pulpit and in the counseling room. We will do that in season, and out of season, in an age of affections and in an age of reason.

This chapter *assumes* that you have read the chapters *What are affections?*, *Why preach to the affections?* and *How do you preach to the affections?* It assumes, in other words, that preaching to the affections is biblical. It assumes that we have a working definition of affections as the leading edge of the thinking-feeling-willing unit of the heart. It assumes that you have a framework for how to preach to the affections.

All we are trying to say here is that our age is at least partly an age of affections, and that therefore preaching to the affections is at least partly helpful. That does not mean that preaching to the affections is not important in other ages (perhaps it is even more important in an age of reason). It does not mean that if our age were not an age of affections, we should not be writing books about affections. It does not mean that we think that preaching to the affections is biblical only because we live in an age of affections. All it means is that affections are prominent on the cultural menu. And so they should be addressed from the Bible.

We are going to analyze:

- what is the same about our age
- what is different about our age
- what we should do about it

What is the same about our age?
Everything of greatest importance. People are still made in the image of God. People are still fallen and depraved. The world and the whole universe is still created by God and sustained by the word of His power. All of reality still throbs to the beating heart of the living God. Jesus is still Lord. The cross is the centre of the universe and of all time and space. The Holy Spirit is the power for ministry, life, change and Christlikeness.

You can stop reading now, and nothing of great importance will you miss. Ecclesiastes is right when it says that 'there is nothing new under the sun' (Eccles. 1:9). Women are still women. Men are still men. Ambition, pride, deceit and all the devilish fears of humanity still dominate the world. The kingdom of God, though, is on the march. The gospel is preached. The church is being built. One day Jesus will return. Every knee shall bow. God will be glorified. Those who resist Him till the end will be cast into outer darkness. The dead shall be raised. Those who love Jesus till the end will join Him in the New Heaven and the New Earth to thrive in an eternity of joy, peace, love and endless glory in Christ.

None of this has changed. None of it ever will.

An Appeal

What is different about our age?

Cell phones. The Internet. Technology. Communication across the globe through social networks like Facebook or Twitter. None of this is essentially different from anything that has come before. Every society finds ways to build its Towers of Babel. But the phones we carry in our pockets have more computing power than our laptops did ten years ago. Text messaging. Email. It's hard to believe it, but when I (Josh) wrote my Ph.D., I wrote it on a laptop with a screen about the size of my cell phone screen now, in black and white. And that was trendy new technology then.

Inevitably, if this book should last longer than six months, what we have just written will be picked over by historians for what we thought was new now. Cell phones! Huh! How quaint! Internet – remember those days when they thought it was still *new*? Hilarious. As historians we *get* this: we read manuscripts of people wondering at how simply *marvelous* it was to be able to write a letter with pen and ink, on scraps of expensive parchment, and then send it across the Atlantic. The sheer miracle of a communication return of a month or so to Scotland from America!

We are not saying these things are new and therefore always will be new. Tomorrow they will be old. That's what it means for something to be new. We are just saying that not everything is exactly the same as it was.

Take books. It is now possible to get a book on a Kindle device in about 15 seconds. That's new. That's different.

We are not saying all of this is better (or worse). We're just saying it is. And it does influence how we do things. For people of a certain generation, we find we can leave them a message, send them an email, and wait and wait. But if we text? Bam! Reply in thirty seconds.

Beneath all these technological changes, at a supporting, complementing, somehow-coming-alongside level is an ideological shift. I (Josh) have written about some of this in far greater detail elsewhere.[1] Since the eighteenth-century Enlightenment, Western culture has been split between the rational and the emotional. The European intellectual elite concluded that 'God' was not ultimately knowable in a rational sense. Everything transcendent, spiritual or divine, then, became a matter of intuition and private devotion.

Both the technological, and the underpinning ideological changes, are major shifts in how society functions. This is not the 1980s. The 1980s communication styles will likely be about as effective as the number of people still living in the 1980s. And that number is not growing.

Again, that does not mean people have essentially changed, that the gospel has changed or that the basic strategy of preaching the gospel has changed. It has not. It does mean that the *way* society is expressing its inherent rebellion against its Creator *has* changed. Jonathan Edwards preached in a wig. He preached sermons with more theological grist than you would find in your average doctoral program at major theological faculties at major universities. His culture was different from ours. Expository ministry in my view is not a cultural factor, but is preaching the gospel like Peter and Paul and Jesus preached it. We want to preach like Jonathan Edwards, but we don't wear wigs when we preach. We want to preach like Paul, but we don't wear sandals when we preach (though maybe flip flops if we're doing a beach mission). We want those to whom we preach to have as much if not more

---

1.   Josh Moody, *Jonathan Edwards and the Enlightenment: Knowing the Presence of God* (Lanham, U.S.A.: UPA, 2005).

theological understanding as your average Puritan congregation in the 17th or 18th century. They do not right now. We are not even sure *we* do right now. We are all on a journey towards greater biblical fidelity and greater gospel godliness.

Everything essential and ultimate is the same. The ephemeral is constantly changing. We are people of eternity preaching the gospel in a season of time.

What we should do about it
Unhesitatingly proclaim the truth of God. Reason in the marketplace of Athens (Acts 17:17), and in the synagogue of Corinth (Acts 18:4). Refuse to capitulate to the Kantian philosophy that says that ultimate truth about God is not accessible. He has been revealed. God is speaking and is not silent. He became flesh. He is risen. He has shown Himself. That not all see it is because the god of this age has blinded their minds, but as we preach Jesus Christ as Lord, God 'has shone in our hearts to give the light of the knowledge of the glory of God in the face of Jesus Christ' (2 Cor. 4:4-6).

Don't believe that emotions are not truth-telling. Contemporary research seems to be showing that our emotional life is more cognitive than older Darwinian theories used to say. Just because certain intellectual elites have sneered at religion for being emotional does not mean we should capitulate and remove emotion. John Calvin (pre-Enlightenment, of course) was right to insist on there being a 'sense of God' in each of us. He was right to insist that self-knowledge could only really come about through the knowledge of God. There is an affective element in biblical ministry.

Don't accept the split between reason and emotion. We are more than a thinking machine. We are also more than an animal acting with no higher nobility than to protect our genetic heritage. Our love, as Christians, transcends that, and we live 'in the Spirit,' not according to the 'flesh.' Oh for more space (and time) to write, but do not accept theories that think that the only truth out there is one discoverable in a test tube. Do not give in to the underlying 'nothing but' assumptions of materialism which says that we are 'nothing but' an animal, any more than you can accept that a Rembrandt is 'nothing but' blobs of paint on canvas.

In other words, use biblical exposition to direct the gospel at the sin behind the sin, the lie behind the lie, the basic heart issues of our day and age. Do not be frightened of technology. Do not become a Luddite. Conversely, do not worship at the footstool of Facebook. Do not become a 'twit' on Twitter. Understand that all cultural mediums of communication carry with them a message. The gospel can be preached through printed material, controversial as that was at the Reformation. The gospel can be preached through microphones, controversial as that was for some when the technology first came out. The gospel can be preached through webpages, controversial as that was. The gospel can be preached through Twitter and Facebook. None of this takes the place of the gathered community of the local church. Obey the word of Hebrews: 'not neglecting to meet together' (Heb. 10:25). And do not think that means a Starbucks latte with your best friend (or two). Join with a local church; submit to its leaders; be a biblical Christian, which means a church Christian, because the Bible never describes a Christian that is not part of a church. To be a Christian and not integrated with a local church is a contradiction in terms, like saying you are married but you do not have a wife. Some of us for a season live with such contradictions at least in the ecclesiological parallel. But church is the expected norm for Christians.

An Appeal

Use technology; do not be used by it. Fast from Twitter. Fast from Facebook. Take a break from email. Understand the implicit message that each medium of communication brings with it. The medium does not equal the message; otherwise, watching pornography on TV would be the same message as watching Billy Graham preach on TV. But TV does have a message that comes alongside whatever it is showing. TV says you can stay home and still listen and watch. Facebook says you can have friends without actually being in the same place as them. Both are truths; they are not *the* truth. They are half-truths, just like reading a book is infinitely less insightful than meeting the author of your favourite book. But that does not mean you do not like reading the book in the first place.

Catch the ideology of our society unawares, like going trout fishing. That 'sense' of God is there. It is rational and emotional. Preach to it. Preach the glory of the gospel of Christ in a way that is rational, but is not only rational. Proclaim Christ so that His glory is sensed. Watch how Jesus does it. Listen to how Paul does it. Read how the great preachers did it. Keep learning until you die, or go hoarse, or are put in prison – and then preach it to the prisoners. Have passion, but not the kind of passion that looks like something out of a bad movie. Have the kind of passion that *you* have when you are passionate about something. If you cry, then weep. If your upper lip twitches just a little, then let it twitch. *Authenticity* is the thing: be who you are in Christ, not who someone else is. Be so captivated by the message of the passage in front of you that you communicate with the unconscious rhetoric of a lover to his beloved, of a beggar pleading for mercy, of a herald announcing the most important news in the world.

Craft your sermons. Craft them so carefully and correctly that when you preach them, each verb and noun sings in unison like a perfectly collaborative choir, or like a drum set in time with a guitar solo. Do not give into the false idea that *spontaneity* equals *spirituality*. Work harder at your Bible work than a barrister works at his court work, than a CEO does at his annual board presentation, than a professor does before a seminal university lecture. If there are four people in the audience, preach as if every single one of them is of infinite importance, for they are. If there are four thousand people, preach as if every single one of them is of infinite importance, too. Do not give in to the cardinal sin of the preacher: pride. Do not give in to the besetting sin of the preacher: discouragement. Lift your eyes to the hills and preach as if you were meant for it, designed for it, set apart for it, and as if it was the most important task in the world.

Above all, 'Preach the Word.' Preach it with passion. Preach it with reason. Preach it with authenticity. Preach it from the biblical text, framed by the biblical text, shaped by the biblical text, and therefore as the very Word of God.

All of this is exactly the same as Paul told Timothy. All of this is different. It is the same in all essentials. It is different in all peripherals. 'Plus ça change, plus c'est la même chose.'

6

A worked example
of preaching to the affections from

Colossians 3:1-11

By this stage, you may be feeling that all this talk of preaching to the affections is rather abstract. So to try and earth what we are talking about, in the next four chapters we want to give you four worked examples of sermons from different genres of Bible literature. As you'll discover, these are far from perfect sermons. They are, however, all genuine sermons in that we have preached them in our home churches. They are also all expository sermons in that they are seeking to preach a Bible passage or verse and let the main point of the passage shape the message. And they all are sermons which try to take seriously preaching to the affections. What we have done is to reproduce the sermon in one font and our comments in another. And along the way, we will pause to show you some of our workings – particularly as they relate to the affections (in bulleted points). As part of that, we will try and show ways in which drawing out these affections contrasts with ways it would be possible to preach the passage in an expository way, but not necessarily affectionally.

Burning Hearts

COLOSSIANS 3:1-11

[1]If then you have been raised with Christ, seek the things that are above, where Christ is, seated at the right hand of God. [2]Set your minds on things that are above, not on things that are on earth. [3]For you have died, and your life is hidden with Christ in God. [4]When Christ who is your life appears, then you also will appear with him in glory.

[5]Put to death therefore what is earthly in you: sexual immorality, impurity, passion, evil desire, and covetousness, which is idolatry. [6]On account of these the wrath of God is coming. [7]In these you too once walked, when you were living in them. [8]But now you must put them all away: anger, wrath, malice, slander, and obscene talk from your mouth. [9]Do not lie to one another, seeing that you have put off the old self with its practices [10]and have put on the new self, which is being renewed in knowledge after the image of its creator. [11]Here there is not Greek and Jew, circumcised and uncircumcised, barbarian, Scythian, slave, free; but Christ is all, and in all.

It's Sunday evening. And your heart is burning within you as you hear God speaking through the Bible. And then the meeting closes with your favourite Stuart Townend song. You leave fired up and longing to live flat out for Jesus. It's Tuesday morning. And that attractive colleague at work or friend at school is wearing particularly summery clothes. And you begin to lust after them as you mentally undress them. Then you get home and scream at the kids for making a mess of the house or at your parents for grounding you. Sunday evening seems a million miles away. And you feel such a fraud, such a failure. Not least because lust and anger are habitual sins in your life.

JOSH: I love this introduction! Why did you choose something from 'inside' the Christian world (Stuart Townend), and at a very 'practical' level (colleague at work), rather than a 'worldview' kind of introduction, or contemporary culture kind of introduction (prevalence of lust among Christians, encouragement of lustful behaviour in contemporary media)? I think what you did works fantastically well. I'm intrigued as to whether you would ever start 'top-down' (worldview) or from culture/media influences? And if so, when would you do which and why?

ROBIN: Thanks, Josh. There are many different ways you can introduce a sermon. I like to try and vary my introductions. Introductions that often work best are ones that 'front-load' the application. In this introduction, for example, I am front-loading application about sins of lust and sins of speech which are the two main areas Paul addresses in Colossians 3:5-9. It is often at the application level that the affections begin to bite, which is why sermons that begin with an indication of how the passage applies are often effective.

Worldview kind of introductions, or contemporary culture kind of introductions can work really well. I chose not to use them here because I wanted to show from the outset that this passage was directly applicable to the hearts of the listeners.

Notice how even in the first two sentences I assume that hearing God speak through His Word is an experiential thing. We need to come to God's Word with the right expectations. If I assume the Bible is boring, the chances are I will find the Bible boring. If, on the other hand, I assume the Bible is dynamite, I'm more likely to have my affections blown up by it as it is read and taught. Notice, as well, how in the introduction I try to tap into that tension between what we long for and how we actually live. This sets up the question of how we can change. And that is the question Paul answers here in Colossians 3:1-11.

Well, if we're a follower of the Lord Jesus, I'm sure we know all too well what that feels like. But how can we change? How can we win the battles of temptation? If we were here last week we'll know that there was a popular answer to those questions kicking around in the church at Colossae. The answer was just two words: 'Do not.' We see it there in 2:21 – just look back to that with me. 'Do not handle, Do not taste, Do not touch.' And that's an answer which is still very widespread today. We hear it in sermons, books and counselling. Like the minister who was preaching on sex under three headings which all began with the letter 'd': 'It's dirty, it's dangerous, so don't!'

That then was the Colossian solution to sin, and a solution many still adopt today. And it seems a pretty good one, doesn't it? Paul acknowledges that in 2:23: 'These have indeed an appearance of wisdom in promoting self-made religion and asceticism and severity to the body...' But in fact it's no solution at all – look at the second half of 2:23: 'but they are of no value in stopping the indulgence of the flesh.' And if we have been struggling with sin for any length of time, we'll know that all too well. Simply telling me 'don't' just doesn't work. So what does work? Well in the first half of chapter 3, Paul gives us a fundamentally different way to change – a way that will work. And that way is all to do with our union with Christ. Our union with Christ leads to our mortification of Adam. Adam was the first man in the Bible. And when he sinned, all humanity sinned in him. So much so that in the Bible, Adam is the representative of sinful humanity. That's what these verses are about: our union with Christ leads to our mortification of Adam.

JOSH: Do you think there are dangers at the other extreme? In other words, is it ever possible to go to the other end of the spectrum to the Colossian false teachers, and instead so emphasise positional realities that we do not ever say 'stop doing that!'?

ROBIN: That's a good point, Josh. I don't think the Bible gives us imperatives ('do this...') without first giving us indicatives ('Because this is true or real...'). In my preaching I always want to work hard at keeping imperatives tied to indicatives. When that connection is broken we end up in moralism or legalism, and lose the gospel.

- See here how I am trying to show both the attraction and the frustration of the Colossian solution to sin. It is a solution that is still peddled today. In its worst form it is moralism. In its best form it is monumental self-will. Many in our churches labour under this solution which is really no solution at all, and seeing that is immensely liberating. It doesn't work, because it is not connected to Christ.

1. OUR UNION WITH CHRIST (VV. 1-4)

Colossians 3:1-4 acts as a kind of bridge in Colossians between the two halves of the letter. The first half is mostly about the person and work of Christ. The second half is mostly about the person and work of the Christian. Of course, those two things are linked. And so in verses 1-4 Paul wants us to understand our union with Christ. Christians are 'in Christ.' 'In Christ' is the New Testament's favourite description of a Christian.

Imagine that in this world there are two giants. Each giant is wearing a broad leather belt, on which are millions of tiny little hooks. And hanging on the belts of these two giants is every man and woman who has ever lived. One giant is Adam, and the other giant is Christ. So if you are a Christian here this evening, do you see what an enormous thing has happened to you? You have been taken off Adam's belt and hung on to Christ's belt. If you are not yet a Christian here this evening, that's what needs to happen to you.

And when that happens, it is just so momentous. Because it means that where Christ goes, I go. If I am in Christ, what has happened to Him has also happened to me. Let's just trace how Paul shows us that we are united to Christ at every stage.

First, we are united with Christ's death. Look at verse 3 – 'For you have died.' Because we are in Christ who died. Then we are united with Christ's resurrection. Look at verse 1 – 'If then you have been raised with Christ.' The 'if' there doesn't mean that there is some doubt. It means 'seeing that' or 'since.' Since we are in Christ who rose, we too have been raised. And so we are also united with Christ's ascension. Look at verse 3 again – 'your life is hidden with Christ in God.' We are in Christ who is now seated at the right hand of the Father. And then we will be united in Christ's appearing. Look at verse 4, because we are in Christ who will return. So do we see then just how deep our union with Christ is. We are united with Him in His death, resurrection, ascension and return, so much so that our life is not simply 'in Christ.' Verse 4, Christ is our life.

- James S. Stewart wrote that 'union with Christ, rather than justification or election or eschatology, or indeed any of the other great apostolic themes, is the real clue to an understanding of Paul's thought and experience.'[1] And yet union with Christ is a strangely neglected doctrine in evangelical circles today, which is why it is not always easy for Christians to grasp this glorious reality. That's why I have used the illustration of the two giants. There are other illustrations that can be used. For example, here is one from the sixteenth-century reformer Peter Martyr Vermigli (1499-1562), in his commentary on the Apostles' Creed:

  > Since he is risen and is our head, we are also risen in him. Tell me, I pray you, when one holds his head above the deep and deadly waters of a fast flowing stream, do we not say that he has escaped death even though his other bodily members are

---

1. James S. Stewart, *A Man in Christ* (London, U.K.: Harper & Bros., 1955), p. vii.

yet below the surface? The same holds true for us, who are all one body in Christ. Our head is risen from the depths of death. Even though we may appear to be overwhelmed in the mortal stream, yet we are risen in him. We must either deny that he is our head or acknowledge that we are members of his body – in which case we are compelled to affirm that our resurrection has begun in his.[2]

Notice as well how being 'in Christ' is profoundly experiential. Albeit inadequately, I tried to get people to feel the magnitude of what has happened to us if we're believers. It's all too easy for preachers, and indeed Christians more generally, to forget how monumental our conversion is.

JOSH: Amen! Is there an affectional element in the apparently mystical idea of being 'in' Christ?

ROBIN: Absolutely. I think that was Spurgeon's point that our faith is a person. Christianity is a living relationship with a living Lord. Being united to Christ transforms us.

When we begin to grasp that, we'll begin to do what Paul says in verses 1 and 2. Verse 1 – 'seek the things that are above.' Verse 2 – 'set your minds on things that are above.' In other words, think about, get excited about where you already are. Christian, you are in heaven. So fix your mind and heart there, not on things here. Think about how you will live there, and that will affect how you will live here. Think of two big circles which overlap in the middle. One circle is the earthly realm. The other circle is the heavenly realm. And if we are in Christ, we now live in the overlap of the circles.

---

2.   I am grateful to Dr Lee Gatiss, Director of the Church Society, for drawing my attention to this.

But Paul is saying that spiritually we actually live in the heavenly realm. So he says, don't set your heart and mind on earthly things. Set your heart and mind on heavenly things. Now I think it's hard to know exactly what this looks like in practice. So let me give some examples of people in the past who have understood the implications of our union with Christ. And just notice how they apply this great truth.

George Mueller was a wonderful nineteenth-century pastor in Bristol. When asked what God had taught him most deeply about life, this is what Mueller said: 'There was a day when I died, utterly died, died to George Mueller, his opinions, preferences, tastes and will, died to the world, its approval or censure, died to the approval or blame even of my brethren and friends, and since then I have studied only to show myself approved unto God.'[3]

'For you have died.'

Rewind eighteen centuries, and we meet John Chrysostom, one of the biggest names in the early church. Once he was brought before the Roman Emperor and threatened with exile unless he stopped being a Christian. To this threat, Chrysostom replied: 'You cannot banish me, for this world is my Father's house.' 'Then I will kill you,' replied the Emperor. 'You cannot,' replied Chrysostom, 'since my life is hidden with Christ in God.' 'Then I will take away your treasures.' 'You cannot, for my treasure is in heaven and my heart is there.' 'Then I will drive you away from every person in the world, and you shall have no friend left.' 'No, you cannot. For I have a friend in heaven from whom you cannot separate me. I defy you. For there is nothing you can do to harm me.'

'Your life is hidden with Christ in God.'

If you go to the crematorium in Oxford, you'll find the grave of Joy Davidman. On it are these words written by her husband C.S. Lewis:

---

3. A.T. Pierson, *George Mueller of Bristol* (Grand Rapids, U.S.A.: Kregel, 1999), p. 367.

A worked example ... Colossians 3:1-11

> Here the whole world (stars, water, air,
>   And field, and forest, as they were
> Reflected in a single mind)
>   Like cast off clothes was left behind
> In ashes, yet with hope that she,
>   Re-born from holy poverty,
> In Lenten lands, hereafter may
>   Resume them on her Easter Day.

'When Christ who is your life appears, then you will also appear with him in glory.'

- Good preaching will have illustrations. Often the illustrations that work best are those that lead into application – what we might call illustrative applications. I have tried to do this above to show the truth of our union with Christ transforms our view of life, death and everything in between. Union with Christ is something to be understood both in terms of our status and our experience. Our status as united to Christ never changes, and the quotation from John Chrysostom is one that emphasises the objectivity of that status. However, it is not only a status to be understood objectively but to be experienced subjectively. The quotations from George Mueller and C.S. Lewis stress the experiential part of our union with Christ. This must not be misunderstood to imply some kind of perfectionism, as if Mueller from the 'day he died' never struggled again with the approval and censure of men. But I think we are sometimes guilty of downplaying the need to appropriate experientially what is true of us objectively.

> Josh: I love these illustrations! How do we make sure that someone who has, perhaps, an over-sensitive conscience is not left wondering whether they have yet 'died'?
>
> Robin: That's a good concern, Josh. I think the key thing here is to point out that dying with Christ is an objective reality, and something that has happened to me regardless of whether I 'feel' it or not.

Friends, consider what an extraordinary thing it is to be united with Christ. And so seek the things that are above – that's where your life is now. But before we think this is just pious thinking, Paul then explains what this will look like in practice. Our union with Christ leads to our mortification of Adam.

2. Our mortification of Adam (vv. 5-11)

Now Adam is not explicitly mentioned in these verses. But I think Paul is referring to him when he talks about putting off the 'old self' in verse 9. Those who now hang on Christ's belt are called to slay Adam. Grasp how violently verse 5 puts it – 'put to death therefore what is earthly in you.' It's what Christians used to call mortification. I think mortification is a really great word. It speaks of killing sin.

- Given what I said about Adam not being mentioned here, perhaps I should have had as my second heading, 'our mortification of our old self.' And rather than the call to 'slay Adam,' I should have said something like 'we need to kill our old nature.' But I deliberately chose that language because I think it is more direct, less predictable, and therefore possibly more likely to raise in our affections a holy hatred of sin and desire to slay it.

Paul then applies his call to mortification in two specific areas: sex and speech. In both areas he lists five particular sins. Look with me at verse 5. Notice how Paul moves from the outward act to the inward motive. So the outward acts are sexual immorality and impurity. That's taking God's good gift of sex and using it the way we want, not the way He wants. It's indulging in or thinking about sex that is not in the context of heterosexual marriage. And the desire to do that comes from inward evil desires, covetousness and idolatry.

As many of you know, my family and I (Robin) recently returned to this country after living in Delhi for six years. There are many things we are enjoying about being back in the U.K. But one thing we're not enjoying is living in what has become a very overtly sexualised society. Even in the six years we have been away, it seems that Britain has become much more overtly sexualised. And so pornography is a massive problem – even for Christians. One of the books I have enjoyed recently is this one by Tim Chester – it's called *Captured by a Better Vision: Living porn-free.*[4] While he was writing the book, Tim did an anonymous online survey about the use of porn by Christians. The results are staggering. He reckons that one in every three Christians regularly uses porn. In a crowd this size, that means as many as are sitting over there. Or in our house group of nine people, statistically at least three members are struggling with porn.

Now the Colossian solution to that is just 'don't'. Don't look at it, don't use the internet in a room by yourself. But 'don't' doesn't work. The strength of Tim Chester's book is that he says we need a multi-faceted approach to the temptation that's all around us. One of the things he highlights is a need to abhor porn. We see that in verse 6. He's also brilliant at identifying the sin behind the sin. What's the sin behind porn? End of verse 5 – idolatry. As we believe the promises of porn more than the promises of God. As we worship the pleasure and power of porn rather than desire the source of all pleasure Himself.

---

4.   Tim Chester, *Captured by a Better Vision* (Nottingham, U.K.: IVP, 2010).

- This is what Thomas Chalmers meant by 'the expulsive power of a new affection.' We tend to deal with the issue of our sinning by trying to manage the action rather than addressing the heart. And when we probe the heart, we see that every sin is ultimately the result of a misalignment of our affections away from Christ and towards something else. The issue isn't pleasure. The issue is what we're finding pleasure in. We need to show people that the fight against sexual sin is ultimately won or lost in the heart. It must be dealt with at the source. And it must be expelled by a more precious and powerful new affection.

There are a couple of copies of this book on the bookstall. Don't feel any embarrassment about buying one – you might be buying it for a friend! But even if you don't buy a copy, let's be killing sexual sin. Sexual sin belongs to our old life in Adam, not to our new life in Christ. So lay siege to your sins. Hunt them down and starve them out by keeping away the food and fuel which is their maintenance and life. But we'll never do that unless we also feed and fuel our soul by considering our union with Christ. And also knowing the forgiveness Christ promises to all sexual sinners – no matter how badly we have fallen.

- Here I am trying to use illustrative language to apply Paul's command to 'put to death what is earthly in you.' Words like 'laying siege,' 'hunt' and 'starve' are not major illustrations but they are word pictures that hopefully stir up in people a holy hatred of sin. Or to give people what Thomas Brooks called it in the title of his book, 'precious remedies against Satan's devices.'

> JOSH: For someone who struggles to come up with such evocative powerful language as you use here, how would you recommend developing the sort of diction which regularly employs this feeling-driven speech pattern?
>
> ROBIN: Read, read, read! And read widely so that we learn from those who use words well, whether that's authors or preachers or whoever.

But before we think that sexual sins are the only ones that matter, Paul goes on to show the sins of speech. Look with me at verse 8. And we're thinking, 'Paul, are you serious?' I mean, what will we talk about on a night out with the boys? Paul is deadly serious. No flippant putdowns. No undercutting. No crude jokes. Apparently the average person spends one-fifth of his life talking. If all of our words were put into print, the result would be this: a single day's words would fill a 50-page book, while in a year's time the average person's words would fill 132 books of 200 pages each! Just imagine that all your words were recorded in a book. How many of them would be angry words, or malicious words, or obscene words, or untrue words? Brothers and sisters, put away all those sins of speech. Let your words be known for their kindness and their honesty. Let your speech be like Christ, not like Adam.

It's not difficult to see what Paul is saying here. What is hard is applying it, which is why I have gone straight to application here rather than give more explanation.

And I think verse 11 gives us a clue to the kind of thing that often causes angry words and lies. So often it's the differences between us that are the source of conflict. But Paul says that those differences no longer matter – 'Here there is not Greek and Jew, circumcised and uncircumcised, barbarian, Scythian, slave, free; but Christ is all and is in all'. Remember that if we hang on Christ's belt, we are united not only to Him but to all those who hang on His belt as well, no matter how different they may seem to us.

So get serious about mortification. Be killing sin or sin will be killing you. Now we might be wondering, if as verse 3 says, we have already died, how can we go on dying? And the answer is that both are needed. We have died with Christ – that was the decisive act. But now we must go on killing sin – that's the decisive attitude.

I recently watched *The Hurt Locker*. It's a powerful film about a bomb disposal team in Iraq. If you've seen the film, you'll remember the bit when the team are ambushed in the desert. There's a fire fight, and the team kill all those sniping on them from an abandoned building. But having won the fire fight, they don't sit back and have their sandwiches. No, they stay at their positions for the rest of the day in case their defeated enemy is still alive and waiting to kill them.

The Christian life is a lot like that. There was a decisive fire fight when the Lord Jesus died for our sins. And in Him we also died. But our defeated enemy is still alive and trying to kill us. So we have to be on constant guard against him. Not giving him the opportunity to attack us so that we sin sexually or in our speech. And that is the position we must maintain not for one day – but for the rest of our lives.

- I used this illustration from a well-known film to try and show how the Christian life is a fight. Although Satan has been defeated, he is not dead but continues to rage against Christ and His people. Also, as British forces are still deployed in Iraq, it's an illustration that comes from a real and ongoing conflict situation, and therefore hopefully not as banal as some film illustrations.

JOSH: Some Christians feel nervous about using movies with violence in them? How do you decide what kind of movie/media illustration to use in which kind of context?

ROBIN: Again, that's a good concern. I try not to use many film illustrations, and certainly would avoid doing so from films which may be off limits for Christians. Given how frequently the Bible uses warfare language to describe the Christian life, I think that war films would be appropriate places from which to borrow to illustrate sermons.

There are two ways to straighten a bent steel bar. One way is to bend it back with brute force. But every time the bar is bent back, the fibres are weakened and soon the bar will break. Well, imagine that our wills are like bent steel bars. The Colossian way to straighten the bar is by brute force. 'Don't'. Soon enough that way will break us. But there is another way, a better way to straighten a bent steel bar. And that is to plunge it in a fire and wait until it glows red hot. Then the bar can be straightened very easily without damaging the fibres.

Friends, that is the Christian way to change our bent wills. By plunging our souls in the fire of the gospel, in the amazing news of our union with Christ so that our red hot souls can be straightened out again and again. When you see that attractive person on Tuesday morning, when you get home on Tuesday evening and you're mad with your kids or your parents, which way will you straighten the iron bar of your soul?

JOSH: It's a brilliant conclusion. Thank you, Robin.

- How to conclude sermons is something many of us find rather difficult. If the introduction is the plane taking off, the conclusion is the plane landing. Some sermons crash land abruptly, others circle many times over the airport and land much too late! Rather than recapping along the lines of 'in this passage we have seen two things,' or introducing a new idea, conclusions often work best when the full weight of the message falls on to one focussed point. That is what I have tried to do here with the illustration of the iron bar. It captures, I hope, the difference between the Colossian solution to sin and the gospel solution to sin. And my prayer is that it would raise in the hearers a desire to plunge themselves in the furnace of Christ and have their hearts warmed, their wills straightened and lives transformed.

7

A worked example of preaching to the affections from

Isaiah 54:5

One of the differences between past and present preachers is the length of the Bible text that is selected to preach. In the past, preachers would often preach on one verse, squeezing it until it yielded all of its juice. In many ways this brought great richness and depth, and allowed the preacher to impress upon congregations one verse. But at times this also led to taking texts out of context which can result in faulty hermeneutics. Largely in reaction to that, preachers today rarely preach on one verse, preferring instead longer preaching units – sometimes even multiple chapters. Whilst we must take careful consideration of context and preaching units, we must not lose either the desire or the ability to preach on one verse. The sermon in this chapter was an attempt to do that. During the service in which this sermon was preached, we had as our Bible reading the whole of Isaiah 54.

Again, the sermon is in another font, and the working is in bulleted points.

> JOSH: I agree about this need to rediscover preaching from a text like this. Thank you for giving us an example of doing it in a way that is faithful to the wider context and is genuinely expositional as well as affectional.

ISAIAH 54:5

> [5]For your Maker is your husband, the LORD of hosts is his name; and the Holy One of Israel is your Redeemer, the God of the whole earth he is called.

We live in a world that is full of disappointment, regret, shame and insecurity. In this week since the general election, many people will be feeling that very acutely. And with another summer of sport now upon us, we need to brace ourselves for yet more dashed hopes and disappointments. But at a more personal level, each of us is affected by the disappointment, regret, shame and insecurity which stalk our world. I wonder in what particular ways we are feeling that right now. Perhaps it's in our marriages. Whether we have never married, or are married, or have been married, many people feel disappointed. Or maybe it's with our children. Or in our jobs. With the recent political and economic earthquakes, there must be many who are feeling very insecure about their jobs right now.

But of course, so often we feel disappointment, regret, shame and insecurity most keenly in our spiritual lives. Disappointment – that we aren't the Christian we would like to be. Regret – over decisions which have spiritually hamstrung us. Shame – caused by sins, that no matter how hard we try, we just can't seem to defeat. And insecurity – as we wonder whether God will really go on forgiving and loving us, or whether if we fail Him once too often, that will be it.

Well, if we're feeling like that, we'll know just how the people Isaiah was writing to felt. Remember Isaiah was talking to God's people at a particularly low time of their national life. The kingdom was divided. The Northern kingdom was being defeated by the

Assyrians, and the Southern kingdom was hurtling headlong towards exile. Just notice how the three synonymous words of shame, disgrace and humiliation are used in this chapter. Notice, too, the three pictures Isaiah uses to describe Israel. She's childless – verse 1, 'Sing, O barren one.' She's a widow – verse 4, 'the reproach of your widowhood.' And she's divorced – verse 6, 'like a wife of youth when she is cast off.'

• In this introduction I am trying to engage with the congregation's experience of living in 'this sad world' as the Heidelberg Catechism so aptly calls it. In this respect, we are no different from God's people in Isaiah's day. So I am using that common context to set up the good news that this verse proclaims. Preaching one verse does not mean that we can ignore the context, and this introduction was an attempt to help people connect experience in twenty-first-century London with that of eighth-century BC Israel. Notice how I used deliberately affectional language – words like 'disappointment,' 'regret,' 'shame' and 'insecurity.' This is what Christians in our churches feel more frequently than we preachers often admit.

JOSH: Same here in Chicago. Is there a danger that strong affectional language, of this particular negative kind, at the beginning of a sermon can set a somewhat melancholic atmosphere from which it is hard to escape the rest of the sermon?

ROBIN: This relates, I think, to the point about needing to vary our introductions, and to let them be governed by the passage or its context. Here I'm using the context of the first hearers (the Israelites in exile) to tap in to the fact that we are still in exile and awaiting the consummation of the kingdom.

So how was Israel to handle the shame, disgrace and humiliation of being spiritually childless, widowed and divorced? How are we to handle the disappointment, regret, shame and insecurity of living in a fallen world? Well, some put their hope in better things. Some give up hoping all together. But the answer verse 5 gives us is that you and I need to put our hope in the character of God. As I'm sure you know, in the Bible someone's name reveals their nature. And verse 5 rings with God's names, all of which reveal God's nature. There are six names altogether – 'Maker,' 'husband,' 'LORD of hosts,' 'Holy One of Israel,' 'Redeemer' and 'the God of the whole earth.' Rather than look at each name in turn, notice how four of the names are coupled together. 'Your Maker is your husband,... and the Holy One of Israel is your Redeemer.' Let's look at each in turn:

1. YOUR MAKER IS YOUR HUSBAND
This incredible juxtaposition of names takes us right to the heart of the gospel, because what we see here is both the transcendence and the immanence of God. I don't want to lose you with big words like transcendence and immanence, but they are great words, even if they need some explanation. When we talk about the transcendence of God, we're talking about His greatness, His otherness. When we talk about the immanence of God, we're talking about His intimacy, His closeness. And I think many of our problems stem either from having a God who is too small or from having a God who is too remote.

So first of all, notice God's transcendence. He is our Maker. The fact that God is the Maker of all things and all people is a big theme in Isaiah. God is the one true God who alone made the world and everything in it. From the enormity of the 100 billion galaxies in the universe, to the detail of each person's unique thumb print, God made it all. Do you know how many times the earth can fit inside the sun? One million times. And our God made both the sun, the earth and all that is in it. And that truth affects the way we treat all of life, whether it's giving dignity to all people because all people are made by God, or whether it's protecting the lives of the unborn or the elderly because we know that all life is made by God, or whether it's our refusal to worship trees or careers or gadgets because they are created rather than the Creator. The fact that God is our Maker should instil in us a holy awe as we consider the enormity of His creative power.

- In his excellent book, *The Supremacy of God in Preaching*, John Piper highlights the great need there is to preach the character of God. He writes:

  > People are starving for God...The greatness and the glory of God are relevant. It does not matter if surveys turn up a list of perceived needs that does not include the supreme greatness of the sovereign God of grace. That is the deepest need. Our people are starving for God.[1]

  Preaching the character of our great and glorious God will touch people's hearts. I think preachers often feel the burden to apply the passage, but in too narrow a sense of the word 'apply'. We think we have only applied the Bible if we have told people what they should or should not do. But 'behold your God!' is a legitimate and affective application to make. And when we do behold Him, our affections are stirred. The affection I am trying to arouse here is one of awe as we consider the majesty of our Maker.

JOSH: Is there a way that we can move from people's *felt* needs to their *real* need of God Himself?

ROBIN: I'm sure there are ways to do this. I think that there are preachers who do this really well, but I'm not sure I'm one of them! I guess part of it is identifying what Bryan Chapell calls 'the fallen condition focus'.

---

1. John Piper, *The Supremacy of God in Preaching* (Nottingham, U.K.: IVP, 1990) pp. 10-11.

That is anything that results from our fallenness. This includes our sin, obviously, but can also include other negative effects of the fall such as loneliness which results from the fall but is not necessarily a sin. It is a consequence of our alienation. It's linking those consequences of sin back to sin itself which helps us move from people's felt needs to people's deepest needs.

But if we were to stop there, our God would be no different from the god of other religions. Other religions also have transcendent gods. But the God of the Bible is not only great – He is also personal. He is not only transcendent – He is also immanent. And His immanence is seen in that word 'husband.' The Bible uses many different pictures to describe God's relationship with His people. But perhaps the one that is used most is that of God being a husband to his bride. In the Old Testament, Israel was frequently called God's bride. In the New Testament, that description is applied to the true Israel – to all who turn from sin and trust in the Saviour. So we who are turning from our sin and trusting in Jesus here this morning are the bride of Christ. Our Maker is our husband.

Just stop and think for a moment what that husband-bride picture means. It means that there is a closeness, a love, an intimacy between us and God that can best be described as the relationship that a husband and wife enjoy. The Bible is essentially a love story as it paints for us a breathtaking picture of God's tender love for His people. Now imagine what those words 'your Maker is your husband' must have meant to those who first heard them. Remember how the rest of chapter 54 describes Israel – as a childless, widowed, divorced woman. But now God is telling Israel that she is a loved and secure bride. So maybe this verse is particularly encouraging to those here who are childless, or widowed, or divorced. Your Maker is your husband. But, of course, even for those of us who are not childless, or widowed, or divorced, this is a great truth because it reminds us of the incredible gospel, that in Christ we are a dearly loved bride.

- Many of us struggle to believe that we are loved deeply and unconditionally by our God. That is because our experience of human love is so often shallow and conditional. Here I am trying to press home the reality that the church is God's bride. As such, we are loved with a steadfast, covenant love which never changes. This is the love S. Trevor Francis described in his hymn as 'love of every love the best.'[2]

> JOSH: I am struck by the way you expound the affection in the passage at this point!

But even as we meditate on the fact that our Maker is our husband, we need to realise that this is not a marriage of equals. No, look at how the verse goes on – 'the LORD of hosts is his name.' We're back to transcendence again. God is so mighty. He is so powerful that He commands the hosts of heavenly angels.

So how do we think about God? I said earlier that many of our problems stem either from having a God who is too small or from having a God who is too remote. So there may be some here whose God is too small. That's why we don't fear Him as we should – because we have domesticated God. He's all matey rather than almighty. That's why we worry about the future – because we don't think God is big enough to deal with the uncertainties of life. I came across this very helpful quotation recently by the pastor and author Kevin DeYoung:

> We obsess about the future and we get anxious, because anxiety, after all, is simply living out the future before it gets here. We must renounce our sinful desire to know the future and to be in control. We are not gods. We walk by faith, not

---

2. S. Trevor Francis, 'O the Deep, Deep Love of Jesus', 1875.

by sight. We risk because God does not risk. We walk into the future in God-glorifying confidence, not because the future is known to us but because it is known to God. And that's all we need to know. Worry about the future is not simply a characteristic, it is the sin of unbelief, an indication that our hearts are not resting in the promises of God.'[3]

And we might add, not resting in the character of God – He is our Maker.

But there will be others here for whom God is too remote. I remember one minister who was asked what he found hardest in ministry. He said, 'The greatest difficulty I have with people before their conversion is persuading them that God is against them. The greatest difficulty I have with people after their conversion is persuading them that God is for them.' Brothers and sisters, if we are trusting the Lord Jesus, then God is for us. He loves us. He is our husband. The Christian life is essentially a love relationship.

So in our Christian walk, we need to hold together both the transcendence and the immanence of God. And what is true individually also needs to be true corporately, which means that when we meet for gathered worship as we are doing today, the songs we sing, the prayers we pray, the sermons we hear should reflect the truth that God is both our Maker and our husband. He is both far and near.

- In our highly individualised Western culture, much of our sermon application tends to be to the individual believer rather than the corporate church. Here I am trying to apply the character of God both individually and corporately. Preaching changes churches, not just isolated people. As well as that, it is important that preachers are theologically aware. We want to preach the Bible not just in an expository way but also theologically. For

---

3.   Kevin DeYoung, *Just Do Something* (Chicago, U.S.A.: Moody, 2009), p. 48.

example, behind that Kevin DeYoung quotation lies a whole lot of doctrine about God's sovereignty and the outworking of that in providence. It would be possible, depending on the congregation, to unpack this some more, although in this case I didn't.

JOSH: This quotation, *'The greatest difficulty I have with people before their conversion is persuading them that God is against them. The greatest difficulty I have with people after their conversion is persuading them that God is for them'* is profound. How have you attempted to persuade people of both realities?

ROBIN: As with everything, we have to trust God's Word to do His work in this area. One of the helpful applications of seeing that God's covenant is at the heart of Scripture is grasping that in the covenant, God says He is for His people. His position towards us is that of blessing us, not cursing us. That is something we need to drive home to Christians again and again, not least because we are surrounded by evidence of God's curse on sin and a fallen world.

But how is all this possible? How can our Maker also be our husband? That brings us to the second half of the verse:

2. THE HOLY ONE OF ISRAEL IS YOUR REDEEMER

Here's how God can at the same time be both transcendent and immanent. Because the Holy One is in the business of redeeming unholy ones like us.

Just like the word 'Maker,' the word 'Redeemer' is a word Isaiah uses frequently. It's a word that comes from the book of Exodus. So whenever an Israelite heard the word 'Redeemer' he would remember how God had rescued them from slavery in Egypt. I'm sure many of us will know the story. If you don't, read the first 15 chapters of Exodus when you get home. It is the greatest rescue act of the Old Testament as God redeemed, literally 'bought back,' His people out of slavery in Egypt by the blood of many lambs.

And then in Isaiah chapter 53 – just one chapter before this one – we read about the blood of another single lamb, a lamb who was led to the slaughter as he bore the sins of his people in his own body. Only we know that this Lamb was not an animal. This Lamb was God's servant and God's Son. The New Testament tells us that this Lamb was the Lord Jesus Christ. The Lord Jesus is the Lamb of God who was slain on a cross for the sins of all who ever put their trust in Him. And it is through His blood that we are redeemed, that we are bought back, that we are purchased.

- In chapter four, we saw how Christ is the sum and substance of the whole Bible, and that we need to preach Him from every part of it. Here you will see how we get to Christ from one verse in Isaiah. We get to Him via the word 'Redeemer' in Isaiah 54:5, and then more fully from the wider context of this verse, namely Isaiah 53. In our experience, it is when we help people make these connections with Christ that the affections begin to be stirred, and love and adoration for Him wells up within us. This brings us back to the definition of preaching we began with in chapter two: Preaching is the God-ordained means by which He meets with His people through His Word and by His Spirit in such a way that His people's eyes are opened to see Jesus and be captivated by Him.

So do we see then how all of this flows from the cross. It all flows from the fact that the Holy One of Israel redeems unholy ones like us. It is because God is our Redeemer that our Maker can be our husband. It's the cross that resolves the great tension that runs right through the whole Bible, the tension of how a holy God can have anything to do with sinful people like us. If we know anything of God's character and if we know anything of our own hearts, we'll feel this tension personally.

A worked example ... Isaiah 54:5

How can we ever come into the presence of a holy God when His holiness will just consume our sinful souls with fire?

And the glorious answer which Isaiah 54:5 gives us and which the New Testament unpacks for us is that God is our Redeemer. The Holy One is in the business of redeeming unholy ones like us. And He does it through the cross, which is why the cross must always be at the centre of all our thinking about God.

Perhaps earlier when we were thinking about intimacy with God it sounded like I was talking about mysticism. And there's no doubt that there is a renewed fascination with mysticism today – just go to any bookshop to see that. But we need to realise the huge difference between mysticism which is pagan and spirituality which is Christian. Mysticism is basically a desire for unmediated access to God. Mysticism says you and I can go directly into God's presence. It therefore bypasses Christ and bypasses the cross. But spirituality is mediated intimacy with God. It always recognises that we need a Mediator, we need a Redeemer if we're ever to approach God.

So friends, beware of any offer of intimacy with God that is unmediated, and any form of Christianity which is not focussed on the cross. We need a Redeemer. And the wonderful truth of this passage is that we have a Redeemer.

But before we get too individualistic about all this, before our horizons are limited to me and my salvation, just notice how the verse goes on. He is called 'the God of the whole earth'. That is, God is not simply 'the Holy One of Israel' – He is also 'the God of the whole earth'. His redemption is for people of every tribe and tongue and nation and language. And one sure way of telling whether we believe this is by whether we have any concern for the spread of the good news of the Redeemer to the ends of the earth.

Well, there are many applications that come out from this verse. Don't let anyone ever con you that theology is not practical. There is nothing more practical than knowing the truth about God. But the two main applications that chapter 54 gives us can be found in the commands of verse 4 and verse 1. 'Fear not' (v. 4) and 'sing' (v. 1). Verse 4 is more obviously an application of verse 5 because verse 5 begins with the word 'for.' In other words, the reason we should not fear (v. 4) is because of the character of God we find in verse 5. It is God who is the guarantee of the existence, growth, and security of His people. As we go into this week, none of us know what the next phone call or doctor's visit might bring. And in this world full of disappointment, regret, shame and insecurity, our only hope is God. So whatever this week holds for you, if you're trusting in Christ, remember that your Maker is your husband. The Lord has redeemed you. The Lord is for you. And nothing you face this week can be greater than the God who loves you. There is no pit so deep but Christ is deeper still. Fear not.

But then also sing, rejoice (v. 1). Chapter 54 which flows out of chapter 53 is full of reasons for rejoicing, chief of which is the character of God. It's been rightly said that the test of a church's faith is not only the wording of its creed, but also the gladness of its worship. Now I know that the way people express joy varies from culture to culture. And we must be careful not to judge who is joyful and who is not. But it would be good to examine ourselves and ask whether both our gathered worship here on Sundays and our scattered worship throughout the week is marked by a deep-seated joy. Because there can be no greater joy than knowing that our Maker is our husband because the Holy One of Israel is our Redeemer.

So friend, where do you look for security in an insecure world? Where do you look for hope in a disappointed world? Where do you look for forgiveness in a shameful world? If the answer is anywhere else than the character of God, our lives will be as fragmented and broken as Israel's was.

JOSH: Is this where you concluded? Talk us through the thinking behind 'landing' the sermon with this sort of concluding 'punch'?

ROBIN: Yes, this is how I concluded. As with introductions, I try to vary my conclusions both in length and in style. This conclusion was brief and punchy, and tried to link back to the themes raised by the introduction.

- When preaching to the affections, it is important to look for the affections the text itself gives us. Here we are given two – one negative, 'Fear not,' and one positive, 'Sing.' Anxiety and an absence of joy are two things many Christians perpetually struggle with. Here I am hoping that God's Word will bite in those two areas. Anxiety is a wrong affection that needs to be banished far from us. But that will only happen when we know the reasons why we should not be anxious, chief of which is the fact that God is *for* His children whom He has redeemed. Instead of anxiety, Christians should be marked by joy. Almost fifty years ago, Martyn Lloyd-Jones made this perceptive diagnosis of joyless Christianity:

> 'The greatest need of the hour is a revived and joyful church... Nothing is more important... than that we should be delivered from a condition which gives other people looking at us, the impression that to be a Christian means to be unhappy, to be sad, to be morbid... Christian people often seem to be perpetually in the doldrums, and too often give this appearance of unhappiness and lack of freedom and of absence of joy. There is no question at all but that this is the main reason why large numbers of people have ceased to be interested in Christianity.'[4]

I know this diagnosis is often true of me, and I think I'm not the only one. So the reality of Isaiah 54:5 needs to impact our affections and stir up in us a holy joy.

---

4. Martyn Lloyd-Jones, *Spiritual Depression* (London, U.K.: Marshall Pickering, 1991).

8

A worked example
of preaching to the affections from

Mark 9:33-50

The goal of this sermon is to show that 'politics' in church life are nothing new and that Jesus in Mark chapter 9 has the answer. In terms of 'affective' elements, throughout the story Jesus holds in His arms a little child. It is His 'visual aid' as He calls His disciples to 'have salt in yourselves, and be at peace with one another.'

MARK 9:33-50

> [33]And they came to Capernaum. And when he was in the house he asked them, 'What were you discussing on the way?' [34]But they kept silent, for on the way they had argued with one another about who was the greatest. [35]And he sat down and called the twelve. And he said to them, 'If anyone would be first, he must be last of all and servant of all.' [36]And he took a child and put him in the midst of them, and taking him in his arms, he said to them, [37]'Whoever receives one such child in my name receives me, and whoever receives me, receives not me but him who sent me.'

[38]John said to him, 'Teacher, we saw someone casting out demons in your name, and we tried to stop him, because he was not following us.' [39]But Jesus said, 'Do not stop him, for no one who does a mighty work in my name will be able soon afterward to speak evil of me. [40]For the one who is not against us is for us. [41]For truly, I say to you, whoever gives you a cup of water to drink because you belong to Christ will by no means lose his reward.

[42]'Whoever causes one of these little ones who believe in me to sin, it would be better for him if a great millstone were hung around his neck and he were thrown into the sea. [43]And if your hand causes you to sin, cut it off. It is better for you to enter life crippled than with two hands to go to hell, to the unquenchable fire. [45]And if your foot causes you to sin, cut it off. It is better for you to enter life lame than with two feet to be thrown into hell. [47]And if your eye causes you to sin, tear it out. It is better for you to enter the kingdom of God with one eye than with two eyes to be thrown into hell, [48]'where their worm does not die and the fire is not quenched.' [49]For everyone will be salted with fire. [50]Salt is good, but if the salt has lost its saltiness, how will you make it salty again? Have salt in yourselves, and be at peace with one another.'

Church politics are fun, aren't they? I remember once talking with a man who had had ample experience of politics both in the world of business and in the church. I asked him what he thought was the difference between church politics and politics in business, and he said, 'Well, at least politics in the world is more honest.' Even at our worst, I suppose, we feel like we need to pretend to be holy.

Now this passage has had many scholars scratching their heads as to its meaning – and how it all hangs together – but really it's quite simple once you have some experience of politics. Jesus is addressing church politics, which are really not fun at all, and actually quite serious. We are to imagine Him, Campbell Morgan tells us, and I think I agree, holding in His arms the child He took in an embrace at the beginning of the passage. Holding that child in His arms, all through the discussion about the demoniac, and the frightening language about those who cause one of these little ones to sin, until Jesus comes to His conclusive statement which is the summary of His whole message here, and His whole approach to this problem of worldliness in a political sense in the church: 'have salt in yourselves and be at peace with one another.' That whole phrase has confused people, too, but basically Jesus is just saying be pure inside, have holiness, have that kind of spicy godliness, but also – and as a result of that – live in such a way that is at peace with each other in the community and in your neighbourhood.

It is a most relevant word, isn't it? I remember someone also once saying to me that the trouble with Protestants is that they are always 'protesting'. But, of course, this kind of competition of who is the greatest, and excluding those who are not 'one of us', not of our club, and thereby causing people to stumble who are simple believers, this kind of thing runs the gamut of denominations and approaches to God. And what Jesus is saying here – this is the main point – is that true godliness may be salty, but it is never competitive: 'Have salt in yourselves and be at peace with one another.'

So let's look at how He develops that theme, that main point, and drives it home with three specific instructions to ensure that we have the true godliness that is salty but is never competitive in this political sense.

First, Jesus is saying:

1. AIM TO BE SERVANT NOT MASTER

This is from verses 33-37. The disciples have been arguing along the road. They are embarrassed when they are asked what they have been arguing about because they know it was not right. They were arguing about who was the greatest. What was going on here was that they were fighting over the succession plan. Jesus had just been teaching them that He had to die. Now – not only ironically, but typically in terms of politics – they were fighting over who was the greatest, that is, who would take over the leadership after Jesus had gone. Jesus must have felt like He was banging His head against a brick wall! He is going to die, He is going to rise again, this is the path that He is taking. Instead of talking about that, what are they talking about? 'Hmm, well,' say Peter, James and John, 'one of us went up to the Mount of Transfiguration so it's going to be one of us, we're the greatest, and anyway,' they carry on, 'you lot couldn't even cast out that demon while we were away,' forgetting it was Jesus, not they who had done it. And of course, the others are incensed, 'Peter, you think you're so great. You're the one Jesus called "Satan", when He said "Get behind me, Satan!" Clearly you're not that great yourself.' And on and on.

ROBIN: Do you often use the imagined conversations like this in your preaching, and if so, what safeguards do you have to make sure they are effective (or even affective!)?

JOSH: I don't often do an 'imagined conversation' because I think it can get hokey, cheesy and a little over the top. On the other hand, there are occasions when the text is so familiar, or it feels so 'distant', as if it occupies some other-world called 'religion' that an imagined conversation like this can be useful. Basically, my guardrails with this approach, to stop it going awry, would be to make sure that the point that the imagined conversation is making is the same as the point of the passage. I don't mind dramatising it a little – this has a long and honourable history, going back to Whitefield, and, of course, Jesus as a preacher – but I want to make sure that the point that the imagined dialogue is making is the same as the point of the text. If that's the case then I'm fine with it.

A worked example ... Mark 9:33-50

And so Jesus asks them what they're arguing about. And they are silent. This silence in Mark's Gospel is frequently used with great rhetoric purposes. The Pharisees are silent when they have nothing to say about His question about healing on the Sabbath. The storm is told to be silent. Here they are silent, with shame. And Jesus says, 'If anyone would be first, he must be last of all and servant of all.'

These are profound words, and we need to reflect on them. First means last, Jesus says. First is last of all and servant of all. This does not mean – ambitious young friends – that the way to get to the top is to make sure you look like a really good servant. You know what I mean, 'I want to sit at the head of the table so let's make a great show of sitting at the bottom of the table, and then perhaps I'll get moved up.' No, it means that what really matters in God's kingdom is not ruling but serving. Jesus is not concerned with who's in charge; He's concerned with who's getting the job done. The Spirit of Christ is not the spirit of the master; it is the spirit of the servant.

Neither, though, does it mean abasing yourself with a false Uriah Heep kind of humility. We're just not to be worried about who gets the glory. We're not to be concerned about who's in control. We're to be concerned about the purpose, the vision, the mission and whether it is being accomplished. This principle really works. It is the death knell of any organisation when people are jostling for position. That's when it's all going pear-shaped. No longer is anyone concerned about whether the homeless are being fed, or the snow being ploughed, or the taxes being put to proper use. They're just concerned with title and prestige. And now we're decaying. This principle here in this passage of aiming to be servant, not master, really works, and it is the great antidote to all politics of whatever kind, churchy or worldly, because these are both really worldly.

But then, great teacher that He is, Jesus does not merely adduce the principle, He illustrates it. He takes a little child in

His arms. Can you see Him? Literally, He enfolds this infant in His arms. He hugs him. Perhaps (they are in the house at Capernaum) it was Peter's child. We don't know. 'Whoever receives one such child in my name receives me, and whoever receives me, receives not me but him who sent me.'

What is Jesus saying here? It's an illustration. It's not literal. Jesus is not saying if you serve in children's Sunday school, you're more holy than if you serve putting out the coffee. He is saying that the little ones – these little ones who are serving, for surely the world and the worldly spirit will see them as naïve as little ones like this child – these little ones, this spirit of service, is what happens when you really accept Jesus and really accept the Father.

Jesus' illustration is still the best one. Sometimes when I am particularly tired with the world, I like to just sit down with a few children. To see a mother with a babe in arms. To see such a little child in Jesus' arms. And just think, yeah, that's what I'm meant to be like. Not childish. Not immature. But naively (as the world thinks) believing that God will take care of me, and my job is just to do what's right and leave the politics alone.

ROBIN: I love the way you pick up and drive home the illustration Jesus Himself uses. Do you think that we preachers are so often searching for great illustrations that we miss the ones that are there in the text?

JOSH: I think it worked with this sermon, though sometimes other passages are less immediately rich resources for contemporary illustrative material. I think reading the older preachers, our forebears, helps us with regaining a sense of the 'imaginative' power of the actual text in front of us. A lot of effective (and not just affective) preaching requires picturing ourselves in the Bible world and then in the world of the people to whom we are speaking, and communicating from one to the other.

Now as I say, I want you to imagine Jesus continuing with that child cradled in His arms, enfolded literally, hugged, as He continues His teaching, for each part of this is driving home His point about what true godliness is like, though salty, never having the party spirit of competitiveness.

And so we come to the second way He is driving this point home, from verses 38-41. Having taught His disciples to aim to be servant, not master, and having begun to illustrate the whole principle with the little child in His arms, He now, child still in His arms, says – driving home the same main point about true godliness and salt, but being at peace – He teaches them to:

2. ACCEPT WHATEVER IS TRULY DONE IN JESUS' NAME

So this is brought up by John, who picking up on the significance of welcoming one of these little children in Jesus' name, remembers that they stopped a person who was driving out demons in Jesus' name because he was not 'one of us.' The significance of this is again church politics. It refers back to earlier in Mark when Jesus' exorcisms were dismissed by his opponents the Pharisees as being done by the prince of demons, being done with the devil's power. Jesus answers that charge by saying that the prince of demons would not be casting out other demons, but the issue of demon exorcism was still controversial. Perhaps John and the others were trying to avoid further confusion by this person who was not one of them going around doing exorcisms in Jesus' name.

And Jesus, of course, answers by saying, well no one can consistently be doing something amazing in my name and then go on to criticise me, so leave him alone. For whoever is not against us is for us. And even someone just giving a simple kind of hospitality of a cup of water in His name will be rewarded, so much more someone doing an exorcism.

Now let's leave the sort of weirdness – for modern secular ears, anyway – of the exorcism alone for a moment and just focus on the principle. What Jesus is saying here is what matters is not whether someone is 'one of us' but whether someone is 'for us.' The first is an issue of tribalism, the second is an issue of mission. The first is an issue of territorialism, the second is an issue of purpose. The first is an issue of control, the second is an issue of vision. The first is an issue of politics, the second is an issue of core values.

- Here I apply this particularly to the local church context.

Very practically, then, this is one reason among many why we as a church have our four core values. You can find them on the webpage. They outline our primary intention to build biblical fellowship, learning, outreach and worship. That's why we have 'proclaiming the gospel' as our vision statement. If someone is for us, and they are doing these things which are basic biblical Christianity, then we not only don't try to stop them, we cheer them on, whether or not they are one of us, a member of our church, of our club, of our network.

I think this teaching of Christ, that we are to accept whatever is truly done in Jesus' name, is of great relevance today. We tend to gather our sense of identity around certain well-known preachers or particular movements or conferences. And when we ask whether we support something, we tend to want to know 'are they one of us?' Did they go to this conference, have they heard this preacher, are they a part of the same club? But we must be both more discerning than that, and less partisan. Someone can both be a part of our club and not share our core biblical commitments, so to go by the standard 'are they one of us' is insufficiently discerning. On the other hand, someone can come from a different network, be a part of a different social class, a different race, and actually share our biblical values.

If you want an illustration of this, again look at the child in Jesus' arms. There he is, cuddled up to Jesus. What matters is whether he is for us. Adopted in the family, maybe. But for us. Are you going to reject the one hanging on to Jesus' little finger because he wasn't born on the same side of the town as you? I didn't think so.

Now the exorcism – well, at the name of Jesus demons flee and fall, and while, I suspect, many exorcisms today happen without the fake fanfare of the TV show, they still need to happen.

Perhaps the demon of drink? I don't mean a drink; I mean alcoholism. Perhaps the demon of anger. I don't mean an angry word; I mean the temper you can't get rid of by losing it. Perhaps the demon of unbelief. Perhaps the demon of loneliness that whispers in your ear 'no one loves me; they don't care about me here; I don't belong; I'm not one of them.' That doesn't matter; the question is: are you for Jesus? For if you are, we'll embrace you like He embraces that little child.

ROBIN: How did people react to this? My hunch is that this kind of application about exorcisms is rare in conservative evangelical churches. Is an understanding of the spiritual battle we are in connected to our understanding of our affections?

JOSH: Interesting, I don't remember any pushback particularly. I thought long and hard about this section. How do you preach an exorcism passage in a contemporary church situation without either seeming to sweep under the carpet the reality of demonic influence, or pandering to those who manipulate such passages to gain control over the naïve, or just dive into sentimentalism. In the end the well-known phrase 'the demon of drink' was a key to me. I used that as a way in to a realisation that somewhere we all probably realise that there are bigger powers at work in our addictions, as evidenced by our language choice with that phrase 'the demon of drink'. Sometimes I think we have to preach the passage as it is, without feeling the need to explain every systematic theological connection, and let the passage's edge hit home as it was designed to do.

Now we come to the last of these ways that Jesus is driving home His point about having salt in yourselves and yet being at peace with each other. Having truth, but not being partisan. Having godliness, but not in a party spirit. Serving, not trying to be master. Accepting all those for us, the same mission and core biblical vision. This now is from verse 42-50, and what Jesus is saying here is this:

3. AT ALL COSTS AVOID STUMBLING AND BEING A STUMBLING BLOCK

Now this is very important because in politics we are tempted to think 'at all costs get to the top', or 'be influential', or whatever. But really, according to Jesus, the thing that at all costs we must avoid is causing someone who is a simple believing Christian, 'one of these little ones,' to stumble and stumbling ourselves.

Now there are a lot of parts to this section that need to be clarified, so let me take them one by one.

First, why are some verses in the footnote of the ESV and modern translations? Very basically, while we believe that the original manuscripts were given without error, and we also believe that God in His sovereignty through manuscript transmission and translation has given us a Bible that is fully reliable in every respect, there is what C.S. Lewis called a 'science' of scholarly decision. That makes it clear that verse 44 and verse 46 (in the footnotes) were added in later by some probably overzealous copyist. Jesus does say, verse 48, 'Where their worm does not die and the fire is not quenched,' quoting from the end of Isaiah, but we don't need to underline it three times, as it were.

Second, what is the connection between verses 49 and 50 and the preceding verses? Jesus is talking about the fire of hell, and then He says 'everyone will be salted with fire' and then carries on talking about salt. Why? There are three possibilities. One, Jesus didn't really say this in this context. Mark simply took a well-known saying of Jesus and put it here by word association with fire. Apart from issues to do with the reliability of Scripture that that interpretation raises, it also should never be our assumption that there is no explanation until we have exhausted all other possibilities. So what are the other possible explanations, and are they persuasive? Well, two, some have said that Jesus here is referring to purgatory. He has been talking about fire. But now He is talking about how everyone will have a refining fire going through purgatory. The trouble with this, very obviously, is that He has not been talking about purgatory, but hell. If we take it to mean then this kind of fire relating to the hell fire, Jesus means that everyone will go to hell, which we know from elsewhere is not true. Three, the last possible interpretation is that Jesus has been talking about the fire of damnation, now He is talking about the fire of personal sacrifice. It seems likely this phrase 'salted with fire', to us unfamiliar, but to them familiar, is a reference to the Old Testament practice of using salt in sacrifices. So Jesus' logic then is avoid anything that would cause a stumbling to others, these little ones, in your religious zeal, over who is greatest, or who is part of your club, for there is a right kind of sacrificial fire, that salted with fire, zeal. That seems the right interpretation. Jesus switches to talking about fiery personal sacrifice for God.

Third, but what does Jesus mean by the salt and the losing saltiness and having peace with each other? Now then that is fairly straightforward. Jesus is saying, have this salt, be pungent, be a moral preservative, don't lose your moral zeal, your evangelistic zeal, your missionary fervour, keep that, don't become insipid and lose your saltiness like the ancient compound salt could do, be salty, be fiery, be salted with fire, and do it in such a way – for this is true godliness – that stays at peace with each other. Do you see what I mean?

Now how does this all hang together, then, these verses 42-50? What is Jesus saying here? The word 'sin' repeated throughout has the image in the original of stumbling block. The kind of sin Jesus means is that which will cause someone to stumble. That's important. Imagine again the little child enfolded in Jesus' arms. It's all been about true godliness being salty, pungent, strong, and one that lives at peace with each other. Aiming to be servant, not master. That was the first way He drove it home. Then accepting whatever is truly done in Jesus' name. That was the second way He drove it home. Now the child is still there, in His arms, and He is saying at all costs avoid stumbling and being a stumbling block.

If you politicise church, if you argue about who is the greatest, if you stop those who are for us because they're not one of us, you could cause a little believing one to stumble because of it. Don't do that. It would be better to be thrown in the sea with a large millstone around your neck. The picture there is of the stone that ground a mill driven by a donkey, so a very large stone, wrapped gruesomely around the neck. It's better for a quick death than causing a little believing one to stumble with these kind of political manoeuvrings. Then He repeats Himself three times – hand, foot, eye. Jesus is not being literal but speaking in the ancient fashion about the physical parts of the body as metaphors of the parts of our personality. These very core parts of our personality, if they're causing us to stumble, cut them off. Perhaps it's something you really want. To stop it would be – we use the same sort of language even today – like 'cutting off your right arm'. No matter; avoid that. Whatever you do, don't cause someone to stumble, for, and I think this is Jesus' logic, if what you want so much, that it's like your right foot, or your eye, or your right arm, if that prestige, or situation, or attainment is that important to you, better not to have it than by trying to grasp for it – arguing along the way who is the greatest, trying to stop someone driving out demons because he's not one of us – for grasping for it could lead you to hell.

ROBIN: Again, I love the way you drive home the illustrations of the text, and drive them home to our hearts' desires, and 'over-desires'.

JOSH: One of the great advantages of preaching from Jesus' words is that He was such a good preacher!

Hell here is the word Gehenna. It was the rubbish dump of Jerusalem. Originally a place where the gross pagan human sacrifices took place, it was destroyed in King Josiah's reign, and became the rubbish dump for the city, with constant burning and worms eating what was not burning, and then its putrid horrible smell and decimation going on and on. A history of symbolic rebellion against God, it became the metaphor for hell. Gehenna, where, as Isaiah says, and Jesus, 'Their worm does not die and the fire is not quenched.' People who don't like hell-fire preaching need to reckon with the fact that Jesus was a hell-fire preacher.

But those of us who are in the church need to reckon with the context of the hell-fire that Jesus is preaching. It is a warning to those disciples arguing about who is the greatest. You are the ones in danger of hell-fire unless you stop, for you are causing one of these little ones to sin. It is a warning to those disciples who try to stop the ministry of those who are not one of them. You are the ones in danger of hell-fire unless you stop, for you are causing one of these little ones to sin.

And so Jesus summarises the whole thing again, masterfully, with His statement 'have salt in yourselves and be at peace with one another.'

If only the church throughout history had paid attention to Jesus' words here, much would be different. We would be fiery. We would be salty. We would be passionate for doctrine. We would be passionate for church. We would be passionate for the gospel. We would not be passionate for who is first or who is in our club. And therefore we would avoid causing little ones who believe in Jesus to stumble, and we would live at peace (and unity therefore) with each other.

9

A worked example
of preaching to the affections from

Revelation 3:7-13

Revelation chapters 2 and 3 provide an opportunity to teach the overarching themes of the book without getting sidetracked by various controversies. These chapters are also an eminently 'preach-able' unit, neatly dividing into seven sections for seven sermons.

REVELATION 3:7-13

> [7] 'And to the angel of the church in Philadelphia write: "The words of the holy one, the true one, who has the key of David, who opens and no one will shut, who shuts and no one opens.

> [8] "I know your works. Behold, I have set before you an open door, which no one is able to shut. I know that you have but little power, and yet you have kept my word and have not denied my name. [9] Behold, I will make those of the synagogue of Satan who say that they are Jews and are not, but lie— behold, I will make them come and bow down before your feet, and they will learn that I have loved you. [10] Because you have kept my word about patient endurance, I will keep you from the hour of trial that is coming on the whole world, to try those who dwell on the earth. [11] I am coming soon. Hold

fast what you have, so that no one may seize your crown. [12]The one who conquers, I will make him a pillar in the temple of my God. Never shall he go out of it, and I will write on him the name of my God, and the name of the city of my God, the new Jerusalem, which comes down from my God out of heaven, and my own new name. [13]He who has an ear, let him hear what the Spirit says to the churches.'"

Today pragmatism rules the roost. Pragmatism is the doctrine, long since established, that the way to succeed is to do what works. This seems so obvious nowadays that the very statement of the opinion appears almost tautologous. Originally a philosophic school stating that the test of truth is its practical results, these days pragmatism is the underlying assumption of much of our lives. And nowhere is it more so than in the realm of religion. We want to know that this God-character is going to have some good results; we want church to be practical.

And this is all reasonable enough, inevitable enough, it appears to us.

But actually, pragmatism is more than this and has more insidious effects than this. It is not just the belief in such truisms of everyday life, such as 'If it ain't broke, don't fix it'. It is not just being 'practical' and 'down-to-earth'. Pragmatism has a tendency to downgrade all endeavours after truth or beauty to the lowest common denominator. If it is not quantifiable, pragmatism tends to end up suggesting it is not true, or at least not worthy of being considered for long. It is pure pragmatism to question the validity of art galleries. After all, are they really producing any practical results? And it is pure pragmatism to defend the validity of art galleries solely on the basis of how many people attended last year. Such statistics are quantifiable, practical and pragmatic in their pure sense. It is pure pragmatism to question the value of intellectual achievements in their purest sense. Universities and professors then become training programs for producing a more effective economy – and if classes and schools cannot match this criterion, then they are appropriately questioned by this all-pervasive pragmatic spirit.

A worked example ... Revelation 3:7-13

The trouble with such things is that while obviously, and clearly, having good results is a test of truth, it is not the only test of truth or worth, and what's more it can be the most elusive test of truth and value. For instance, the good results of teaching someone about higher mathematics or the beauty of a painting are not readily quantifiable. They are, nonetheless, there. Most of the greatest – and let it be said, practical – technological advances of the last 50 years or so came about as a result of research into pure theoretical mathematics, research that was funded not for a pragmatic reason but out of a principled commitment to the advance of human knowledge.

In other words, one cannot always tell what is going to have the best result. And if the best, most practical result is the only and the dominant guiding criterion, then much that will actually produce good results – if left to its own – will fall by the wayside. What room is there for beauty, truth, love, the higher virtues, in a purely pragmatic universe? Unmitigated pragmatism is the strip mall of truth.

ROBIN: This is an engaging introduction, Josh. It feels quite long. Do you vary your length and style of introduction?

JOSH: Yes, I do. I think the question 'how long should your introduction be?' is a bit like asking 'how long is a piece of string?' The answer to both is: It depends! What you are trying to do with an introduction is to surface the human need related directly to the intention and theme of the passage so that when you come to exposit more directly the text, people are ready to put in the effort to listen. How long it takes to establish that connection is different on every occasion. Sometimes you can do it with a sentence or two. Sometimes it requires a story. Sometimes, as here, there is an undergirding contemporary attitude that takes a little longer to tease out. But starting with the application, as you so helpfully guided us to do earlier in this book, is usually the best approach in one way or another.

It is interesting to note, then, that the church of Philadelphia, one of the two churches in these seven letters of Revelation to receive praise without criticism from the lips of the Lord Jesus, is a church that, pragmatically-speaking, has, verse 8, 'little power.' Yet it is commended. It is a model of a healthy church. Unlike Smyrna, the other church that receives pure praise from Jesus, it is not only excellent in its current faithfulness, but it has excellent possibilities for future usefulness. It is in fact a church with enormous pragmatic opportunities – it has 'an open door' (v. 8). And yet none of this comes from a pragmatic commitment but rather from a principled commitment to – again, verse 8 – the 'word'. It is this that they have held on to or 'kept', which is emphasized in verse 10. Literally, that is, 'Because you have kept my word about patient endurance'. It is this Word of Jesus, the Word of God, that is the controlling principle of excellence which defines the Philadelphian church.

So what I think this passage is teaching us – see what you think as we get into it – is that an excellent church is a Word-driven church, or a church that holds on to, or keeps, the Word. And it does so in three ways. First, it tells us that this is what honours Jesus. Second, it tells us that this is what creates opportunities. Third, it tells us that this is what works.

1. FIRST, THEN, AN EXCELLENT CHURCH IS A WORD-DRIVEN CHURCH FOR THIS IS WHAT HONOURS JESUS.

Keeping God's Word is always here connected to what honours Jesus. In verse 8, keeping the Word is connected to having not denied Jesus' name: 'You have kept my word and have not denied my name.' The name of Jesus is His character, His reputation, His honour. They have kept His Word and have not denied His name. Because they have done this, Jesus Himself, so honoured, will bring others to acknowledge that He has loved them. Verse 9: 'I will make them come and bow down before your feet, and they will learn that I have loved you.' Since, verse 10, they have kept the Word of His endurance, He will also keep them from 'the hour of trial.' And then, verse 12, so reputable of Jesus are they that it is on them that Jesus will write His name, the name of the city of God, and the name of God. The Word is what exalts the Lord Jesus: His name and His love are connected to the church that holds on to the Word.

We think of the Word of God as something intellectual. For Jesus, it is personal.

ROBIN: Josh, I think this truth in many ways gets to the heart of what we're saying in this book: that the Bible is personal and relational, not simply propositional. Why do we tend to think of the Word of God as something intellectual rather than personal? In our preaching, how can we mitigate against this?

JOSH: I think this goes back to the basic development of our culture in the West so that we tend now to assume that knowledge, truth and facts belong more to the objective/rational/empirical realm – or if we do not like that approach, we tend to deny that there is any truth at all. We have a split distinction between truth as merely factual and objective on the one hand, or – in other tendencies in our culture – truth as merely personal and experiential. You can see this distinction or split in multiple areas of contemporary life. In some ways, the church reflects these distinctions. Biblically, truth is ultimately a person: 'I am the way, and the truth, and the life' (John 14:6). Also, the Word is likewise ultimately a person: 'In the beginning was the Word' (John 1:1). We should not read those statements as in any way militating against a hard-line conviction of propositional truth – far from it. Each of them is a propositional statement! But we need to learn to school ourselves to think of all truth as related to who God is.

As far as our preaching goes, I think the main practical takeaway in this regard is to be clear in our own minds about this matter, and then that conviction will percolate through our own distinct personalities as we preach. So knowing that the Bible is personal and relational, not simply propositional, does not mean that we need to pretend to be certain sorts of people as we preach, or that we need to speak more loudly or cry more often. We need to be ourselves as we are when we are deeply 'affected' by the truth. That will then communicate through our preaching authentically, without putting on a show of being a certain sort of person or type of individual.

It is His Word. It is, in fact, the Word of His endurance. That phrase ('my word about patient endurance', v. 10) may indicate a specific command in Scripture to endure patiently. It may indicate the personal suffering that the message of Christ involves. It is the Word of His endurance, or of His suffering: it is the Word of Christ, the suffering servant. They have held on to that and not rejected the cross of Jesus that the Word of Jesus speaks about. Those who reject the Word soon enough downplay the cross and before long deny the name. It is the Word of Jesus that witnesses to the exclusive Lordship of Jesus – His being the only way of being saved – His cross, His sufferings, His patient endurance, winning for us who believe salvation from death and hell, this Word witnesses to the name. And if we have a low view of Scripture, soon enough we will have a low view of Christ. But if we hold onto the Word, we honour Jesus. It is His Word. He gave His blood for it. It is personal, not just intellectual.

We think of the Word as something dry and objective and removed from worship. In fact, the Word honours Jesus. It exalts Him. It shows His love and His name. It is a personal Word, a Word of love, and hence a Word of honour for Jesus.

You have heard it said that the Bible is God's love letter to us. It is also Jesus' personal name. The Bible is spelt 'JESUS'.

But Bible study is so boring, people say. It is so dry. And expositional ministry – such as we are doing now, taking a text and explaining it and applying it – is so passé. What we need is technological pyrotechnics; that will bring them in! What we need is more entertainment! Why do we need to explain the Bible? We all know what it says anyway. We need surveys; we need results. The last thing in the world we need is the Bible; let's keep it on the shelf. Let's have it on the podium, and let's have brief motivational messages about life which occasionally refer to a bit in the Bible, and then we can excite everyone and sort of connect God to the excitement. That'll work.

Well, actually, it won't work, as we'll see. Neither will it honour Jesus. It cost Him his life, this Word. Keeping to it may cost us something. Franklin Graham wrote a book called *The Name*[1] in which he describes how he was criticized for praying in the name of the Lord Jesus at the inauguration of a president of the United States. However gracious we attempt to be, there can be something deeply offensive in the exclusive claims to worship of the Lord Jesus Christ. Sticking to what the Bible says about Jesus may cost us patient endurance, too – a cross, too, as it cost Jesus the cross. But if we honour Jesus, if we love Jesus, we will keep the Word at the heart of our churches. It is a defining test of our relationship to Jesus. You can't say you respect me and twist my word for your ends. Neither can you say you honour Jesus and not let His Word set the direction of your life.

2. FIRST, THEN, WORD-DRIVEN BECAUSE IT HONOURS JESUS. SECOND, AN EXCELLENT CHURCH IS A WORD-DRIVEN CHURCH BECAUSE THIS IS WHAT CREATES OPPORTUNITIES.

Verse 7: 'The words of the holy one, the true one, who has the key of David, who opens and no one will shut, who shuts and

---

1. Franklin Graham, *The Name* (Nashville, U.S.A.: Thomas Nelson, 2002).

no one opens.' Verse 8: 'I have set before you an open door, which no one is able to shut.'

This 'open door' has been given various interpretations by scholars. Some have said it is an open door of prayer. Others have said it is an open door of missionary expansion. Others still have said it is an open door access to God through Christ, an open door of salvation. Others again have thought that it is an open door to entrance to the kingdom when Jesus returns. I think it may well be all of these.

Let me explain. The phrase 'open door' is 'open' to various possible uses. A little later in this chapter it means being willing to repent, verse 20, 'Behold, I stand at the door and knock. If anyone hears my voice and opens the door, I will come in and eat with him, and he with me.' At the beginning of Revelation chapter 4, it means the extraordinary access that John was given to the throne room of heaven, 'After this I looked, and behold, a door standing open in heaven!' The apostle Paul characteristically used the phrase for missionary opportunities. He asked the Colossian church to pray that a door would be opened for his ministry; he gave thanks for an open door to the Corinthian church. This is how the phrase is used in the book of Acts as well.

The point here in Philadelphia is that the messianic fruition was in the hands of the church and no other religious institution. Christ holds the 'key of David', verse 7, a reference to Isaiah 22:22. He can open the door. He has opened the door for the church. And verse 9, those who think they have understood the message of the Old Testament, who claim to be the inheritors of the promise of Abraham, but have not combined that with faith in Jesus and His Word, will come to realise the genuineness of the Christian church and worship with them the Lord Jesus: 'I will make them come and bow down before your feet, and they will learn that I have loved you.' Incidentally, if you're ever tempted to think that the Bible is anti-Semitic, it is helpful to remember that the people writing it were ethnically Jews (and Jesus was a Jew). The point is not ethnic; it is religious. Who has real access to God? Who has the power of the keys of the kingdom? Who is engaging in true worship of God? It is the Christian church through the gift of Jesus.

So the 'open door' here could mean anything that characterises those on the inside track with God. It could mean freedom in prayer, it could mean access to God, it could mean salvation, most particularly as it is explained here in verse 9 to mean evangelistic success. They will 'bow down', that is the word used for 'worship'; they will become worshippers of Jesus too, join with them, and together enjoy the fruit of the messianic kingdom of the Lord Jesus who has the key of David, and through whom heaven itself is an open door.

ROBIN: I notice that you're not afraid to use 'worship' language in this part of your sermon. I think in the U.K. at least, many of us are wary of that word because of the way it has been hijacked. How do you think we can use Bible words biblically? And does that connect to the affections in any way?

JOSH: Interesting, I wasn't consciously trying to be teaching within that context of the worship conversation, but simply reflect what I found in the text. Perhaps that's the best way to deal with any such potentially thorny issues! I try to get out of the way and let the text speak. If it hits the nail on the head, so be it.

I do think the use of biblical words in biblical ways is a more significant matter than I had realized until fairly recently. I find in church circles more and more people seem to use 'Christianese' in ways that seem to imitate biblical ideas, but when you scratch beneath the surface a little bit, it is actually not the same as what the Bible means. I do think this leads to confusion, and perhaps turns people away from the truth when they don't like what they think the Bible means by something, when really it is not what the Bible means at all. I don't consciously try to redefine people's terms, but I do try to make sure I use words accurately. A key tool for any teacher is to be careful with his words and watch carefully their unintentional resonance throughout the whole semantic range of a particular word. But I don't deliberately go after particular words that are being misused, or if I do, I only do so occasionally as warranted by the text in front of me. I suspect that this sort of 'redefinition' of biblical words is probably another reason for why good expositional preaching is to be the main diet of a church. Gradually, truth and clarity will 'drip feed' through us all as we look carefully into the Bible together.

3. AN EXCELLENT CHURCH IS A WORD-DRIVEN CHURCH BECAUSE IT HONOURS JESUS, BECAUSE IT CREATES OPPORTUNITIES, AND THIRD, BECAUSE THIS IS WHAT WORKS.

Verse 10: 'Because you have kept my word about patient endurance, I will keep you from the hour of trial that is coming on the whole world, to try those who dwell on the earth.' Verses 11-12: 'I am coming soon. Hold fast what you have, so that no one may seize your crown. The one who conquers, I will make him a pillar in the temple of my God. Never shall he go out of it, and I will write on him the name of my God, and the name of the city of my God, the new Jerusalem, which comes down from my God out of heaven, and my own new name.'

These verses initially appear nearly impenetrable, but are well illustrated by an insight into the scene of the city of Philadelphia itself.

Like Sardis, Philadelphia had been devastated in the catastrophic earthquake of A.D. 17. Sardis was initially worst hit, but Philadelphia, being nearer to the epicentre of the quake, suffered aftershocks, it seems, subsequently for a long time. In fact, the residents of the city took to living outside of the city in the open plain in order to avoid the danger of constantly unpredictably falling debris. Philadelphia was a city famous for its religious and athletic festivals such that it was called 'little Athens'. It was also well-known for its wine. Right on the edge of the volcanic material of the area, with volcanic rock being good for growing vines, it established wealth through its wine trade. It was also a gateway city. It had two important trade routes running through it, and may initially have been established as a missionary city of Greek culture and language.[2]

All these diverse local conditions are helpful for illustrating what's going on here. For in A.D. 92, the emperor enacted a devastating command whereby a large proportion of vines of the local area were destroyed. Perhaps to encourage the growing of wheat instead of vines, this came near to destroying the economy of Philadelphia, for it – while being a perfect region for growing vines – was not predictably good soil for wheat.

The 'hour of trial', then, in verse 10 may refer to this. It is a peculiar expression. Literally, it is 'the hour of the trial'. It is something specific in mind, and something that went over the whole of the world. The phrase there was probably used to indicate the inhabited earth as distinct from the non-Roman world. It was an issue for the empire. It is quite possible then that this hour of trial is the hour of the trial that was unwittingly released on the Roman world. It was particularly barbaric, for no one, not even conquering armies, destroyed vines or olive trees because they took so long to grow to maturity, and their destruction could mean the starvation of the people.

---

2. This is Ramsay's characterization in Ramsay, WM, *The Letters to the Seven Churches* (Peabody, U.S.A.: Hendrickson, 1994) p.287, although this is a characterization questioned in Hemer, CJ, *The Letters to the Seven Churches of Asia in Their Local Setting* (Grand Rapids, U.S.A.: Eerdmans, 2000), p. 174

The 'crown' is the well known athletic wreath given to the victor in athletic conquests, especially appropriate for 'little Athens'. The promise, 'never shall he go out of it', was especially heartwarming for a people who had in recent history had to flee an earthquake-devastated city time and time again.

In other words, what Jesus is saying is that this spiritual, principled commitment to the Word works in practice. They have held onto the Word; He is going to hold on to them come hell or high water, or judgement or famine.

It works now, verse 10, during the famine; they will be held onto and protected. Not taken out of the situation – like Jesus prayed for his disciples that God would not take them out of the world, but that they would be protected from the evil one – not taken out of the situation, but kept from the specific hour of trial about to arrive.

It works for the future, too, verses 11 and 12. 'I am coming soon,' Jesus says, quickly in the sense of imminently, not necessarily immediately, 'coming soon'. This is referring to Jesus' second coming. Hold on to what they have (What do they have? What are they holding onto? The Word!) so that they do not lose their crown, the crown of victory in this testing conquest for their souls. And he who does hold onto the Word, he who does 'conquer', will be made a 'pillar'. That is secure, stable, not shaken any more like they experience those aftershocks: 'Never shall he go out of it'. He will have the name of God, of the city of God and of Jesus Himself invested in him. That is, those who have kept Jesus' Word and therefore honoured Jesus' name will be privileged to have that name, that honour, that commitment relayed to them for eternity in the city of God. The writing of the name is an Old Testament image picked up in various ways indicating ownership. Like we write our name on something to say it is ours, so Jesus is saying that because of our commitment to Him and His Word and His name, He is committed to us now and for all eternity.

It is a wonderful passage. The excellent church holds onto the word for this honours Jesus, it creates opportunities, and it works even in the practicalities of economic challenge as well as eternal destiny.

Strangely enough, however, a few short years after this was written the excellent church of Philadelphia was struggling. Ignatius, passing through on his way to martyrdom to Rome, noted that the influx of new converts from Judaism had created a tendency to despise the New Testament Word, the apostolic Word, the Word of Jesus that had been their great achievement. And, a little later still, a sect called the Montanists rose up to shake the Christian world with their claim to a new word, a prophetic inspiration, which led to the denial of the Word of Jesus. Strangely enough, it is possible that it was Philadelphia that was the birth place of these Montanists.

ROBIN: I like the way you root the text in its historical context as well as its biblical one. What would you say to those who are nervous of doing this for fear that it gives the impression that we 'need' extra biblical material to interpret and preach Scripture?

JOSH: That's a great point! It's the part of this sermon that made me most nervous, too. I did as much research as I could on this to make sure I was fairly confident that I had my facts right. I then presented it as tentatively as I could to make sure I was communicating that this was on a different level of certainty than the Bible. I then communicated it as more of an 'illustration' than an 'explanation' of what was happening. I do think that is sometimes helpful, and certainly permissible.

Like those you mention, though, who are nervous of giving the impression of 'needing' extra biblical material,

---

I do this fairly rarely. I know well that historical background material is long debated in the secondary literature, and I don't want that shifting sand to determine interpretation of the text. If I find the meaning of the text as it stands is then illustrated by historical background, then I may on occasion do as I did here in this sermon – present it illustratively. But I will not do it the other way around (determine the meaning of the text by the latest theory about historical backgrounds). Anyone who is tempted to do that should look into the history of history: it's surprising how much the past apparently changes in the interpretative gloss of historians through the ages!

How could this be? We can see the seeds of the trouble even here. The Montanists claimed that the promise of the coming kingdom of the Lord Jesus would be filled right now on earth, and claimed that the city of God had descended from heaven. The Judaizers sought God speaking only in the Old Testament, the Jewish scriptures. Both forgot to hold onto the Word, which is why verse 11 is so apropos: 'Hold fast what you have.' Do not give way to a supercharged spirituality that claims to overwrite the once for all faith delivered to the saints. Do not give way to a legalistic moralism that denies the saving Word of Jesus in favour of the law.

Instead, hold onto the Word.

Conclusion

Preaching to the affections without sentimentality

So to conclude, we believe that preaching to the affections is biblical and important. It is something that neither of us does perfectly! We still have much to learn. I (Josh) have greatly enjoyed reading Robin's chapters and have benefited from them already. I (Robin) am so grateful to Josh for giving us such a helpful understanding of the affections and how that impacts our ministry.

The basic point we want to make is that preaching to the affections can be done in a way that is not sentimental, is not emotionally manipulative, but connects to the whole heart of a person – the thinking-feeling-willing unit. We want to say that that approach is biblical. And we want to say that it is particularly helpful in our day. Our guess is that many of our heroes – past and present – have done this intuitively and instinctively. It has certainly been our experience listening to them preach that our 'hearts have been warmed' and that our affections have been moved. Under God's providence, we would probably not be writing this chapter if that were not the case. I (Josh), for instance, have been influenced for life by being bussed down to hear Dick Lucas preach on Sunday evenings. I (Robin) had the immense privilege of sitting under Jonathan Fletcher's ministry and training for four years. Neither of us feels any great need to shift things in a totally different direction. We are just considering a touch on the tiller in relation to this biblical category of the heart and preaching to the affections. We want to learn from the Bible to preach a little better in that way, and find models in church history and around the world of godly preachers who can help us raise our game in this regard.

How *can* you preach to the affections without sentimentality? Perhaps that almost seems like a contradiction in terms! Remember that we are defining affections in a certain way – that is as the leading edge of the heart, the thinking-feeling-willing unit, of the core, the centre, of the human personality. So being affectional does not mean being sentimental. We should not lower our commitment to biblical scholarship, critical thinking, careful exegesis, one iota. Instead *with that* in place, and constantly emphasised, we should *direct* that message, according to the authentic genuine message of the passage, towards the hearers so that they (and we) have our hearts warmed, changed and moved towards life, to the praise and glory of God.

This is not pietism all over again (pietism used in a negative sense; we certainly want to be pious in a biblical sense!). This is not being sentimental or excusing sloppy thinking or sloppy preaching as long as it makes people excited. We need balance, biblical balance. As you can tell from this book, we are not there; neither of us feels remotely that we have arrived. What we have written here is our best attempt, at this time, at this moment, to say 'let's preach to the affections.'

If that is a message that is biblical, we trust it will catch fire in our hearts. And be useful for God's people. And ultimately be honouring to God.

Soli Deo Gloria.

PT RESOURCES

RESOURCES FOR PREACHERS AND BIBLE TEACHERS

PT Resources, a ministry of The Proclamation Trust, provides a range of multimedia resources for preachers and Bible teachers.

Teach the Bible Series
(Christian Focus & PT Resources)

The Teaching the Bible Series, published jointly with Christian Focus Publications, is written by preachers, for preachers, and is specifically geared to the purpose of God's Word – its proclamation as living truth. Books in the series aim to help the reader move beyond simply understanding a text to communicating and applying it.

Current titles include: *Teaching Numbers, Teaching Isaiah, Teaching Amos, Teaching Matthew, Teaching John, Teaching Acts, Teaching Romans, Teaching Ephesians, Teaching 1 and 2 Thessalonians, Teaching 1 Timothy, Teaching 2 Timothy, Teaching 1 Peter, Bible Delight, Burning Hearts, Hearing the Spirit, Spirit of Truth, Teaching the Christian Hope, The Ministry Medical* and *The Priority of Preaching*.

Practical Preacher series
PT Resources publish a number of books addressing practical issues for preachers. These include *The Priority of Preaching, Bible Delight, Hearing the Spirit* and *The Ministry Medical*.

Online resources
We publish a large number of audio resources online, all of which are free to download. These are searchable through our website by speaker, date, topic and Bible book. The resources include:

- sermon series; examples of great preaching which not only demonstrate faithful principles but which will refresh and encourage the heart of the preacher

- instructions; audio which helps the teacher or preacher understand, open up and teach individual books of the Bible by getting to grips with their central message and purpose

- conference recordings; audio from all our conferences including the annual Evangelical Ministry Assembly. These talks discuss ministry and preaching issues.

An increasing number of resources are also available in video download form.

Online DVD
PT Resources have recently published online our collection of instructional videos by David Jackman. This material has been taught over the past 20 years on our PT Cornhill training course and around the world. It gives step by step instructions on handling each genre of biblical literature. There is also an online workbook. The videos are suitable for preachers and those teaching

the Bible in a variety of different contexts. Access to all the videos is free of charge.

The Proclaimer

Visit the Proclaimer blog for regular updates on matters to do with preaching. This is a short, punchy blog refreshed daily which is written by preachers and for preachers. It can be accessed via the PT website or through www.theproclaimer.org.uk.

'Teaching' titles from Christian Focus and PT Resources

Teaching Numbers
ISBN 978-1-78191-156-3

Teaching Isaiah
ISBN 978-1-84550-565-3

Teaching Amos
ISBN 978-1-84550-142-6

Teaching Matthew
ISBN 978-1-84550-480-9

Teaching John
ISBN 978-1-85792-790-0

Teaching Acts
ISBN 978-1-84550-255-3

Teaching Romans (1)
ISBN 978-1-84550-455-7

Teaching Romans (2)
ISBN 978-1-84550-456-4

Teaching Ephesians
ISBN 978-1-84550-684-1

Teaching 1 & 2 Thessalonians
ISBN 978-1-78191-325-3

Teaching 1 Timothy
ISBN 978-1-84550-808-1

Teaching 2 Timothy
ISBN 978-1-78191-389-5

Teaching 1 Peter
ISBN 978-1-84550-347-5

Spirit of Truth
ISBN 978-1-84550-057-3

Teaching the Christian Hope
ISBN 978-1-85792-518-0

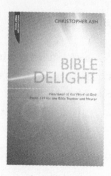

Bible Delight

ISBN 978-1-84550-360-4

Burning Hearts

ISBN 978-1-78191-403-8

Hearing the Spirit

ISBN 978-1-84550-725-1

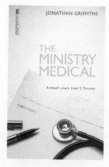

The Ministry Medical

ISBN 978-1-78191-232-4

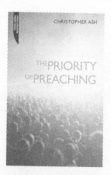

The Priority of Preaching

ISBN 978-1-84550-464-9

ABOUT THE PROCLAMATION TRUST

We exist to promote church-based expository Bible ministry and especially to equip and encourage biblical expository preachers because we recognise the primary role of preaching in God's sovereign purposes in the world through the local church.

Biblical (the message)
We believe the Bible is God's written Word and that, by the work of the Holy Spirit, as it is faithfully preached God's voice is truly heard.

Expository (the method)
Central to the preacher's task is correctly handling the Bible, seeking to discern the mind of the Spirit in the passage being expounded through prayerful study of the text in the light of its context in the biblical book and the Bible as a whole. This divine message must then be preached in dependence on the Holy Spirit to the minds, hearts and wills of the contemporary hearers.

Preachers (the messengers)
The public proclamation of God's Word by suitably gifted leaders is fundamental to a ministry that honours God, builds the church and reaches the world. God uses weak jars of clay in this task who need encouragement to persevere in their biblical convictions, ministry of God's Word and godly walk with Christ.

We achieve this through:

- PT Cornhill: a one year full-time or two-year part-time church based training course

- PT Conferences: offering practical encouragement for Bible preachers, teachers and ministers' wives

- PT Resources: including books, online resources, the PT blog (www.theproclaimer.org.uk) and podcasts

Christian Focus Publications

Our mission statement –

STAYING FAITHFUL

In dependence upon God we seek to impact the world through literature faithful to His infallible Word, the Bible. Our aim is to ensure that the Lord Jesus Christ is presented as the only hope to obtain forgiveness of sin, live a useful life and look forward to heaven with Him.

Our books are published in four imprints:

CHRISTIAN
FOCUS

Popular works including biographies, commentaries, basic doctrine and Christian living.

CHRISTIAN
HERITAGE

Books representing some of the best material from the rich heritage of the church.

MENTOR

Books written at a level suitable for Bible College and seminary students, pastors, and other serious readers. The imprint includes commentaries, doctrinal studies, examination of current issues and church history.

CF4•K

Children's books for quality Bible teaching and for all age groups: Sunday school curriculum, puzzle and activity books; personal and family devotional titles, biographies and inspirational stories – because you are never too young to know Jesus!

Christian Focus Publications Ltd,
Geanies House, Fearn, Ross-shire,
IV20 1TW, Scotland, United Kingdom.
www.christianfocus.com